NORTHAMPTONSHIRE
AT WAR 1939–45

NORTHAMPTONSHIRE AT WAR 1939–45

KEVIN TURTON

Pen & Sword
MILITARY

First published in Great Britain in 2017 by
PEN & SWORD MILITARY
An imprint of
Pen & Sword Books Ltd
47 Church Street
Barnsley
South Yorkshire S70 2AS

Copyright © Kevin Turton, 2017

ISBN 978 1 47387 667 5

The right of Kevin Turton to be identified as Author of this work has been asserted by him in accordance with the Copyright, Designs and Patents Act 1988.

A CIP catalogue record for this book is available from the British Library.

All rights reserved. No part of this book may be reproduced or transmitted in any form or by any means, electronic or mechanical including photocopying, recording or by any information storage and retrieval system, without permission from the Publisher in writing.

Printed and bound in England
By CPI Group (UK) Ltd, Croydon, CR0 4YY

Typeset in Times New Roman by SRJ Info Jnana System Pvt Ltd.

Pen & Sword Books Ltd incorporates the Imprints of
Pen & Sword Archaeology, Atlas, Aviation, Battleground, Discovery, Family History, History, Maritime, Military, Naval, Politics, Railways, Select, Transport, True Crime, Fiction, Frontline Books, Leo Cooper, Praetorian Press, Seaforth Publishing, Wharncliffe and White Owl.

For a complete list of Pen & Sword titles please contact
PEN & SWORD BOOKS LIMITED
47 Church Street, Barnsley, South Yorkshire, S70 2AS, England
E-mail: enquiries@pen-and-sword.co.uk
Website: www.pen-and-sword.co.uk

Contents

Acknowledgements		vi
Introduction		vii
Chapter 1	1939 – Germany Advances	1
Chapter 2	1940 – Britain at Bay	17
Chapter 3	1941 – Defeats and Setbacks	40
Chapter 4	1942 – Seeing it Through	54
Chapter 5	1943 – Turning the Corner	70
Chapter 6	1944 – Hitting Back	85
Chapter 7	1945 – Victory	104
Chapter 8	Aftermath	117
Index		123

Acknowledgements

I would like to thank all the authors named below whose work and knowledge has aided my research, Northampton Libraries and Maureen Yule for her unstinting support in helping to put this book together.

Northamptonshire at War	Northamptonshire Libraries
The Turn of The Tide	Arthur Bryant
Islip, Past, Present and Future	Islip Parish Council, 1995
Oundle's War	Michael Downes
The World at War 1939-45	Readers Digest
The Northamptonshire Regt	Northampton County Borough
World War II	Christopher Chant, Brigadier Shelford Bidwell OBE, Anthony Preston, Jenny Shaw

Northampton Libraries

Shared Memories	Joyce Haynes
A History of Kettering	R.L. Greenall
1889–1989 Government & County	Jonathon Bradbury
Airfield Focus	John N. Smith
Old Kettering – A view from the 1930s	Tony Ireson

Introduction

After the carnage of the First World War, people quite rightly believed that there could never be a second, greater conflict. The cost, both in financial terms and human lives, had been so ruinous to all the countries involved that to even contemplate the idea was surely absurd, or so the argument ran. But as history now records, whilst the countries of Europe had dismantled their armies and rebuilt their industries, they had paid little heed to the defeated Germans. The Treaty of Versailles, supported by the victors, had forced Germany to give up 25 per cent of its territory and pay reparations for the death and destruction the war had caused. In turn, this had caused rampant inflation across Germany in the early Twenties, the collapse of many businesses and massive unemployment. It had also aided the growth of the National Socialist German Worker's Party and the rise of its leader, Adolf Hitler.

It is probably fair to say that for most people living in Northamptonshire at the start of the 1930s, Hitler's was not a name easily recognized or known. The rise to power of Hitler and his odious entourage went largely unnoticed until around 1936. He had become a feature of newsreels and newspapers before then as Germany had begun its own recovery, but for most he was no more than a passing interest. Yet by this time he had managed to rise from obscurity to prominence after the Germans, under his leadership, had remilitarized the Rhineland. This area of Germany had essentially been declared neutral under the terms of the Versailles Treaty, mainly because it was land west of the Rhine that bordered Belgium, Luxembourg and the Netherlands. In 1919, it had been occupied by what were known as the entente forces – France, Russia and Britain – and any move to reclaim it would have been seen as inflammatory. When Hitler took it back, possibly to test the West's reaction, it raised the prospect of the war no-one had ever envisaged; a war which at that stage still seemed unnecessary and avoidable. While it rang a few alarm bells, it did not cause a sudden rush to re-arm, although in December 1936 the British government did take the precaution of forming the ARP (air raid precaution unit). Westminster was all too well aware, even at that stage, of the consequences of any future war on the British people.

From this point on, people across the county became ever more aware of the growing threat Germany had begun to pose. They began to read of Hitler's plans for the reunification of Germany, how he wanted what he saw as the ethnic Germans of eastern Europe brought into the German Reich, how he had successfully managed to re-arm and of his appalling treatment of the German Jews, the latter being held responsible by Hitler and his government for the savage terms of the Versailles Treaty.

Any further doubts people had of the growing threat from the other side of the Channel were dispelled at the start of 1938. In February of that year, Germany made its first moves toward reunification by threatening Austria. Some six million Germans, most displaced by the terms imposed on Germany at the end of the Great War, lived there. Hitler wanted them back under German rule and began to apply pressure to Austria's chancellor, Kurt von Schuschnigg, threatening to take them back by force. The chancellor decided to ask all Austrians by referendum if they would agree to Germany's request. Hitler demanded it must not go ahead, and on 11 March closed the frontier with Austria, massing troops along its length. Austria's chancellor then looked to Britain and France for help, but none came and he resigned. A new chancellor was brought in and the Anschluss (political or economic union), as it was termed, began. In April, the German army marched unopposed into Vienna, cheered on by huge crowds.

Throughout the summer of 1938, Hitler, with Austria now under German control, turned his attention toward West Czechoslovakia's Sudetenland. At a series of orchestrated rallies, he demanded it be returned to the German nation, arguing the three million or so Germans residing there had also been unfairly annexed by the terms of Versailles. The drums of war were starting to beat long and loud.

In Britain, Prime Minister Neville Chamberlain, all too well aware of the threat Hitler now posed, attended an outdoor meeting in July held in the grounds of Boughton House, Northamptonshire. Over 15,000 people from across the county attended, and during the fifty-minute speech he addressed the issue of a European war.

It was a war, he made clear, that he wanted to avoid at all costs, but one he was not afraid to fight – 'if our liberties were in danger we would fight again'.

To that end, he told the crowd, the government had already begun to take steps to ensure the country would be well-placed to defend itself, including increasing the strength of the Royal Navy, vital if the country was to maintain the level of imports it needed to ensure continued stability.

The speech was well received, though it is doubtful many felt reassured. War had begun to seem almost inevitable by this time, and when, in late September, Hitler addressed the Nuremberg Rally, it appeared unavoidable. Hitler's speech, widely reported, was a culmination of the threats and demands that he had made throughout the summer, an emotive, combative rant in which he repeated his insistence that the Germans in the Sudetenland be allowed to decide their own futures, but this time with more venom than at previous rallies. Whether orchestrated or not, the address had caused riots and discontent across Czechoslovakia, sufficient for the heads of Europe to realize, perhaps for the first time, that the German juggernaut was about to roll across them all if they did not react.

On 29 September 1938, Chamberlain flew to Munich. There, he joined French Prime Minister Edouard Daladier and Czechoslovakian President Edvard Benes. At a meeting brokered by Mussolini, Italy's Fascist Prime Minister, they joined Hitler to discuss a way forward. There really was none. Just after midnight, they reluctantly agreed to his demands and handed over 11,500 square miles of Czechoslovakian territory. The Sudetenland was back in German hands. The following day, Chamberlain held a separate meeting with the German dictator, during which they discussed ways to 'remove possible sources of difference'. This resulted in his return to Britain clutching the infamous bit of paper, which he waved in front of the waiting cameras, and which he hoped would bring peace: 'I believe it is peace in our time.'

Churchill disagreed, and in the House of Commons was quite damning of what the Prime Minister had achieved: 'England has been offered a choice between war and shame. She has chosen shame, and will get war.'

Of course Churchill was right. Peace was a forlorn hope. On 1 October 1938, Hitler's troops marched into Czechoslovakia. There was only one destination for his armies to go after that to complete his reunification plan: Poland. There, as the whole of Europe well knew, the western half of the country had been under German control until Versailles, and Hitler was already casting an envious eye on its borders.

In Northamptonshire, trench digging had already started. Across the county, an army of volunteers had begun to dig around any densely populated area in an attempt to create rudimentary air raid shelters, including around Northampton's racecourse. They recognized all too well the sounds of war when they heard them, no matter how distant.

CHAPTER ONE

1939
Germany Advances

As 1939 dawned, sandbags began arriving in Northamptonshire. Despite the Prime Minister's belief that war could be avoided, it had been decided to begin the process of protecting key buildings. By the end of January some 24 million sandbags had been distributed across the county. Council offices, police stations, railway stations, access to some shopping areas and all other buildings deemed vulnerable to air attack, disappeared behind a defensive wall. Elsewhere, women began to sign on for the Women's Voluntary Services for Civil Defence (WVS). Originally formed back in the summer of 1938 as an organization intended to recruit women to work under the ARP banner, its scope had been widened and now it looked for women to form a civil nursing reserve or learn how to drive ambulances and take over roles in hospital supply depots. Hugely successful throughout the war, the organization had already seen over 30,000 women volunteer countrywide.

In March, a major blackout exercise was carried out across Northamptonshire involving all the emergency services. This involved the setting up of searchlights around the county, operated by men of the 4th Battalion Northamptonshire Territorial Regiment, who had been converted into the 50th (anti-aircraft) Battery, Royal Engineers. Their role was to use the lights to probe the night skies, seeking enemy aircraft (in this instance supplied by the RAF), whilst air raid sirens alerted industry and in particular the steel works at Corby and Islip to dim their furnaces to prevent detection from the air. On the ground, police and fire services simulated the likely effects of a gas attack, and in various locations a variety of experimental aircraft 'listening devices' were set up to ascertain their effectiveness in identifying high-altitude bombers. Street lights were extinguished, traffic bollards were masked (as were traffic lights) and shop lighting turned off. A taste of things to come but widely accepted by most as a necessity, the exercise was deemed a huge success in the analysis that followed twenty-four hours later. Despite the disruption, it no doubt brought home to people just what war would mean to their daily lives and that war was coming ever nearer. Plans were then put in place to repeat the exercise in July, August and the rest of the year if necessary.

At around the same time of this first exercise, Hitler marched his army into Slovakia after the country declared independence under German protection. This effectively gave Germany a base from which to launch any future invasion of Poland, and had not been agreed upon at Munich. Prime Minister Chamberlain immediately protested, but refused to consider any stronger action. Hitler then began to demand Danzig (Gdańsk) be returned to German rule. Poland refused to accede any territory, but realized just how perilous their situation was. They were unequivocal in their refusal to bow to Hitler's demands and made it clear that any attempt at seizing it by force would result in all-out war. Britain and France then promised Poland immediate military assistance should that happen. Europe held its breath.

So did Britain, but unlike much of Europe it had time on its side, and intended to use that time wisely. Planning for the probable war had begun to dominate government thinking. They knew this would be very much a people's war, unlike the one they had fought twenty years earlier; a war where Zeppelins were replaced by modern bomber aircraft, capable of carrying a greater payload, flying greater distances and with the technology to bomb far more accurately and to more devastating effect. Sandbagging buildings would only do so much. What was needed was a way of protecting civilian populations should Germany launch air attacks using the air power they knew it had developed. Therefore, investment was made in the manufacture of Anderson shelters.

Back in November 1938, Chamberlain had placed Sir John Anderson in charge of the Air Raid Precautions (ARP). He had commissioned an engineer, William Paterson, to create a shelter that was cheap, easy to construct and could be built in people's back gardens. Measuring 6ft 6in (1.95m) x 4ft 6in (1.35m) and made of six curved steel sheets with a steel plate at each end, the shelter he designed could be half buried in the ground, with earth thrown over the top and the entrance protected by an additional reinforced steel shield. Capable of housing six people at one time, who could sleep overnight if required, it was the perfect solution and became known as the Anderson shelter.

In Northamptonshire, some 7,000 shelters had already arrived by the start of the summer, and delivery continued up until the end of the year. Demonstrations on how to build them effectively were held on Northampton's racecourse, and their importance readily accepted by most households. Essentially, they were free to homes where the weekly income was less than £5 a week, and could be bought by those with higher incomes for £7, but there were some problems and not everyone benefitted. In low-lying areas, for example, they were prone to flooding, and at night they were

Anderson Shelter (Northampton Central Library).

dark, damp and noisy. They were also of little use to the terraced streets without gardens. Nevertheless, the shelters were seen as an essential acquisition in early 1939, even if their effectiveness was still to be measured.

Those who possessed them accepted the perceived safety these shelters offered both to themselves and their families in the hope, no doubt, that they would never be needed. But the inevitability of war must have seemed to grow with every passing day, reinforced by the constant supply of negative news pumped out by newspapers – national and local – alongside radio broadcasts and cinema newsreels, each in their own way beginning to ratchet up the tension as they reported on the ever-changing European situation. This, of course, resulted in a renewed public interest in politics, with meetings better attended than at any time since the start of 1914, everyone looking for either reassurance after the Prime Minister's Munich meetings of the previous year, or an affirmation that should war come, Britain was equipped to win it. In Northamptonshire, one of the most-attended speakers was Kettering's prospective Conservative candidate, John Profumo. After overtures had been made to Hitler by America's President Franklin D. Roosevelt in an attempt to dampen down talk of a new war, he held a public meeting at Rothwell's Tresham Hall. The huge audience arrived to hear his views on Hitler's response, as he saw it, and how the international situation was being viewed by the political class. The public were possibly disappointed but probably not surprised when, in a long speech, he offered little by way of reassurance. A consummate orator, after reviewing the state of affairs in Germany, Profumo told his audience more or less what they already knew; in part, I would suggest, because there was nothing new to add to what was already in the public arena. Hitler's response to America's peace overtures had already been widely reported. Nothing he had said at the Reichstag had given rise to renewed hope that Germany would not continue to pursue its expansionist aims. Neither had Hitler's speech aggravated an already grievous situation, so Profumo's unremarkable, perhaps even anodyne address was understandable at this stage of 1939.

But it was not only a potential war with Germany that was on people's minds in the county. There were other pressure points, and one in particular was in Ireland. The IRA had already given notice of intent at the start of the year in a letter to the Prime Minister. By the summer, their activities were being widely reported in the press as they bombed their way across London and then carried out a major atrocity in Coventry. Widely reported across Northamptonshire, their bombing of Coventry, a neighbouring city, raised fears of additional attacks within the county, this time by home-grown terrorists with easy access to all areas of the shire. As well as the menace posed by a Europe at war, there was also the threat from across the Irish Sea and the furtherance of a conflict believed to have been concluded after southern Ireland had gained its independence in 1921.

With all this going on, people were looking for a little light relief. It came at the start of the Annual Hospital Week, with civic parades and marching bands. In Rushden it was intentionally colourful, with flags, decorated banners, uniforms and a marching procession made up of the various emergency services, the Brownies, ARP and local councillors. All then congregated around the parish church to listen to the Temperance Band as they participated in the county-wide attempt to raise £100,000 for Northampton's general hospital. Kettering followed on with its Carnival Day. Intending to raise funds for its own hospital, a huge procession assembled in Hawthorne Road before weaving its way through the town, culminating in the choosing of a carnival queen followed by a band concert, acrobatic displays, side shows and a variety of entertainments. Similar events then occurred across the county, every one of them attracting huge crowds and without doubt raising the funds needed. It was a brief interlude in what was proving to be a very testing year, a chance for people to forget about the impending war for a while and have a little fun, something that would be in short supply in the years to come.

Elsewhere, attention was drawn toward the resurrection of the Women's Land Army, which was being formed for a second time. Hugely successful by the end of 1918, it had been decided to reform the organization in anticipation of men working in agriculture being called up by the Army. A register was started around June for those women who were prepared to give up their ordinary jobs to take on farm work should war break out. After a slow response, mainly due to the ongoing uncertainty, women across the county began to register. By mid-summer, forty-five had enrolled. If nothing else at this stage, it began to build confidence in the ability of farms to continue producing food if and when manpower was reduced.

People across the county were also being encouraged to sign up as National Service Volunteers. The government had already issued a handbook and enrolment forms, which were freely available at all employment exchanges, post offices and banks. In essence, this was a call for volunteers to come forward across Northamptonshire and join the ARP, an organization which at this time covered a wide variety of posts and was essentially a civil defence organization where people were allocated roles as auxiliary nurses, clerks, welfare workers, special constables, auxiliary firemen and of course air raid wardens. The scope of the organization was extremely wide and, as time went on, incredibly effective. But in the summer of 1939 it desperately needed people to understand its remit and enrol to become a crucial part of supplying the services needed all across the shire. The county had formed a National Service Committee made up of men and women from all parts of Northamptonshire, and in particular its villages. Their role was to organize and recruit volunteers and report to the county council on how well or badly the service was doing every month. At the start of June 1939, whilst awareness of the scheme was growing, they were reporting that shortages still existed across most areas. In order to improve this awareness, therefore, it was decided to organize a tour by a broadcasting van for a fortnight. The aim was to take the van across the county, obviously stopping at towns but perhaps more importantly travelling to as many villages as possible, in order that it could address the largest possible audience. Whilst this was an area of obvious importance, it was the armed services that were suffering the greatest manpower shortages. The 4th Battalion Northants needed 250 men to bring it to full strength, the RAF required fourteen pilots, thirteen more in the Observer Corps and sixty-one extra ground staff. The Royal Navy, on the other hand, was recruiting better than expected. So clearly there were issues that needed addressing, but quite rightly it was felt that the armed services were better left to the government to deal with, whereas the ARP and its various sections were considered more of a local issue and, being voluntary, far easier for people to understand the need for. In the case of the armed forces, manpower issues quickly became irrelevant as the year progressed.

Elsewhere in the county, sandbagging continued apace. Still seen as crucial by both government and council, but costly and slow, Northampton's Borough engineer, R.A. Winfield, had invented a mechanical method of filling bags at the West Bridge Depot. This meant more buildings could be incorporated into the planning of defence, though not everyone was happy with their increased use. Problems had already been reported of bags bursting when wet, and in places rats had been sighted burrowing into bags around some business buildings. It was felt these issues were simply teething problems, and overall their effectiveness in air raids would far outweigh any environmental concerns, so sandbagging continued across the whole county.

Another key area that councils in Northamptonshire were beginning to examine in close detail was hospitals. Government had made funds available to improve the county's hospitals where necessary, in order that they would be better able to handle casualties. This meant they needed to have first-class surgical facilities and make any necessary changes to fixtures and fittings to accommodate these needs. The Ministry of Health had appointed a medical officer, whose role it was to visit all the county's medical facilities to assess their effectiveness and enforce any necessary changes. Extra bedding and equipment had already begun to arrive in the county, and was sent on to those hospitals with the greatest need. Once complete, they would be considered Grade 1 hospitals able to cope with all emergencies. Essentially, this meant Wellingborough, Northampton and Kettering would be expected to handle the worst of any casualty situation.

Alongside these changes, and in many ways equally important, was the shoe industry. This was a key employer in Northamptonshire, with – according to figures released in early summer 1939 – 12,000 employed in Northampton, 9,286 in Rushden, 850 in Raunds, 4,800 in Kettering, 1,600 in Desborough and Rothwell and 500 in Burton Latimer. Overall, the industry was in a reasonably strong position at this time, despite having had to cope with an increase in foreign imports over the previous two or three years. Crucial for its future, as had been the case during the First World War, it would be called upon to supply the Army if war ensued.

As Northamptonshire, like counties across Britain, began to move to a war footing, reports coming out of London began to show just how complex the international situation was becoming. Meetings had been ongoing with Russia since the spring in an attempt to keep them on the side of the western Allies. Ministers had also been meeting with Turkey's government and holding talks in London with officials from Palestine. In Italy, Mussolini had been doing a little sabre-rattling of his own and had annexed Albania after sending in 100,000 Italian troops. In turn, this had threatened Romania and Greece, who looked to Britain and France for security. The British Prime Minister, along with his French counterpart, reacted by offering them the same guarantee he had offered Poland. Mussolini then signed what became known as the Pact of Steel with Hitler, in essence guaranteeing mutual support in the event of any future war. So, as each morning's newspaper landed on the doormat, it was clear to most people that events were unfolding at an alarmingly fast rate.

Too fast in many ways, and not wanting to be caught unprepared, the government decided to react to this ever-changing political scene by announcing the implementation of the Military Training Act. Essentially, this was the first stage of conscription. The Act called for all men between the ages of 20–22 to enlist, the intention being to train them over a six-month period and then discharge them into an active reserve, calling the militiamen, as they became known, back into the Army should a war start. The British Army at this time was a small, professional body made up of Regular Army and Territorials, hence the need to increase its numbers significantly if it was to be embroiled in another European war.

By August it was becoming clear more would probably need to be done, after talks with Russia failed to build an alliance after they ignored British overtures and instead signed a non-aggression pact with Hitler in Moscow. This resulted in all Army reservists being called back to barracks and mobilization notices being sent out to all members of the Observer Corps. Airforce control centres would have to be manned continuously, as they were key at this stage to the RAF as an early warning system of air attack. The corps' role was to identify aircraft, calculate their altitude, direction and number, then pass that information back to the fighter group headquarters. They were the only way of tracking aircraft once

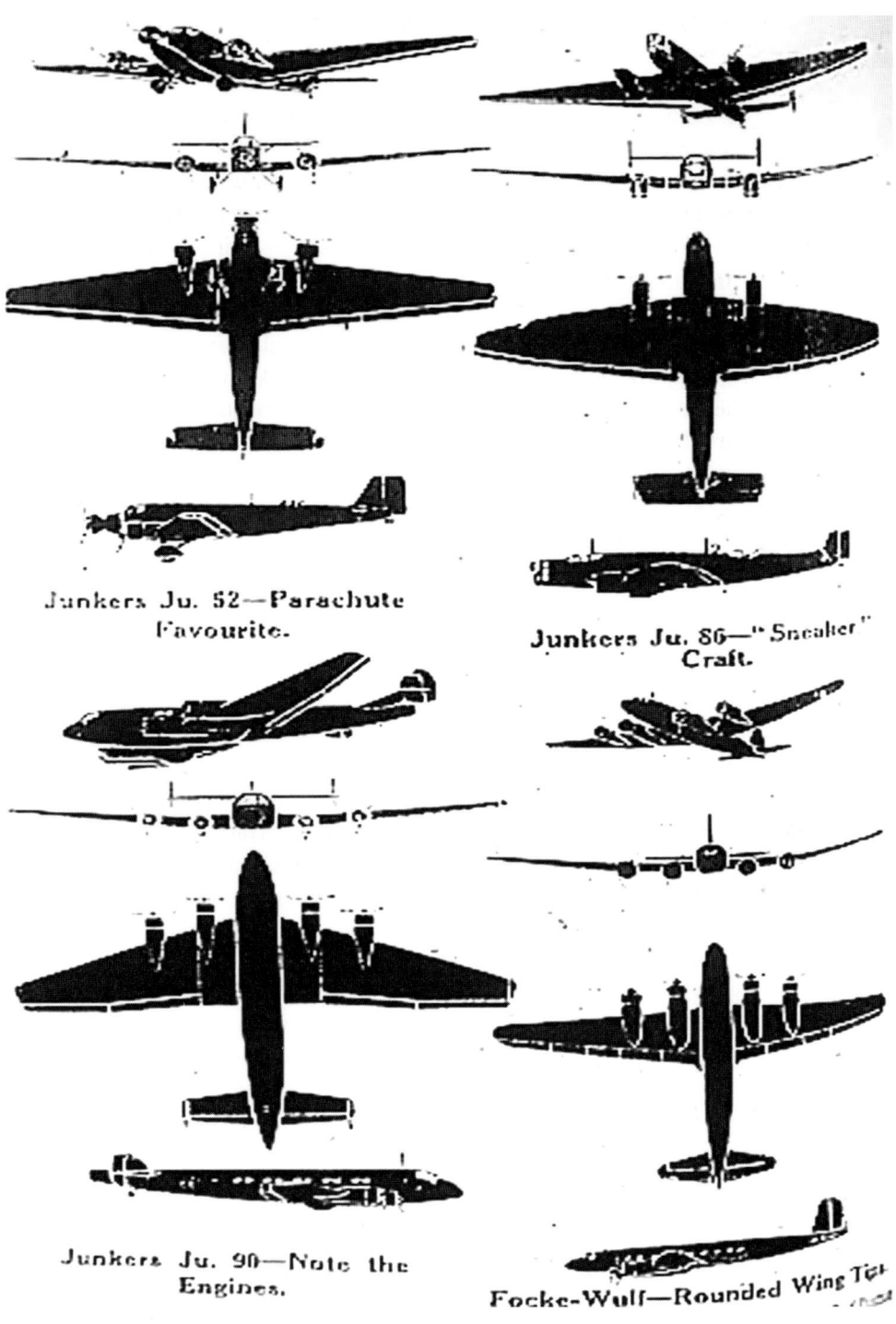

Aircraft identification used by the Observer Corps.

they had crossed the coastline, and without them, air raid warning systems would have been ineffective. Northamptonshire was well covered, with stations at Earls Barton, Brackley, Olney, Raunds, Kettering, Benefield, Oundle, Daventry and many other locations scattered around the surrounding counties.

A final attempt was made at this point to stop Germany's relentless race to war when Pope Pius XII stepped in and, along with Britain and France, called for Hitler to settle his differences with Poland by negotiation. It was never going to happen but it did cause Germany to pause. On 31 August, during this lull, Poland sent its ambassador to meet with Hitler's foreign minister, Von Ribbentrop. It came to nothing.

On 1 September, German troops attacked all along the Polish border. Hitler addressed the Reichstag, and in an inflammatory speech he blamed Poland and their refusal to allow Germany to reclaim Danzig as the reason for military action:

> Poland has directed its fight against Germany. It did not think of keeping its obligations to the minorities. Germany has always kept its obligations to minorities. We have done so in every territory.

This meant that the port and a corridor of land along Poland's western borders, which had been under German rule prior to the First World War and lost as a result of the Versailles Treaty, was to be reclaimed. War with Britain and France was an inevitable consequence, though Chamberlain did his best to avoid it. When he addressed the Commons twenty-four hours later, it was to tell the House that he had issued an ultimatum to Hitler requesting his army withdraw in order to facilitate discussions with Poland. But Parliament was in no mood to accept another Munich-style meeting with the German leader. At 11 am on 3 September, the Prime Minister made his now famous broadcast to announce that the British Empire was at war with Germany. France followed on six hours later. By the end of the day, The National Service (Armed Forces) Act imposed conscription on all men aged between 18–41, except for those medically unfit or exempted by the industry which employed them, be it mining, farming, medicine, engineering or the like.

From this point on, plans laid down months earlier began to be implemented, starting with a compulsory enforced blackout in every town and village and the speeding up of the government's evacuation order. This meant children under the age of 14 living in what had been deemed a vulnerable area were to be sent off to the countryside, or abroad. This could either be done privately, where a family evacuated children to stay with friends or relatives, or officially through their school. Northamptonshire had been designated a low-risk area and was one of the counties allocated to receive children, mainly from the south of England. Billeting across the county being compulsory, with fines imposed on any household that refused to participate. Children began arriving at the various railway stations across the county from 1 September onwards. These trains had no toilet facilities and carried no food, so the children were sent off with whatever food their families could pack up for them, and arrived carrying their gas masks and wearing luggage labels around their necks giving their name and the name of their school. Upon arrival in the county, they were taken to a communal eating place, usually a village hall, parish hall or school. From there, after being fed, they were allocated homes or chosen by their new foster families, based on their perceived usefulness. Families taking in these evacuees were paid 10s and 6d (52p) a week for one child. If they took in more than one, they were paid 8s. and 6d. (42p) per child. If they took in an adult – some children were accompanied by their mothers and, in many cases, teachers – they were paid an additional 5s. (25p) to cover the extra costs for water, sanitation and accommodation. In the first week of September, some 20,000 evacuees arrived in the county, and by the end of the month that had risen to over 45,000. It was not always a successful match for either party. Within weeks, complaints were being reported, particularly from homes where accompanying mothers had been taken in. Many were criticized for being lazy, unable to cook well, bad cleaners and smokers who liked a drink. Similarly, complaints bounced back from some evacuees sent into rural areas who found themselves being forced to live in tents. Dissatisfaction on various levels eventually caused many to simply return home, and by the start of 1940 probably more than half of these arrivals were back amongst their own families.

    Whilst all this was ongoing, a decision was taken by Northampton County Council, as part of their hospital and health planning, to incorporate into the ambulance service haulage vans and converted motor horse boxes across the county. The intention was to supplement the emergency services by calling on their owners to release these vehicles to carry wounded, should there be high casualties at any time due to enemy bombing. Their owners, of course, would be duly compensated for their use.

Perhaps unexpectedly, the day after the Prime Minister's broadcast all cinemas closed. Too many people in one place was considered too great a risk in the event of an air raid. It caused much debate, cinema being one of the greatest sources of entertainment, particularly for a public at war. They reopened just one week later after their owners agreed to show slides warning their audiences if an air raid warning had sounded. It was felt this would allow any who wanted to leave to do so without interrupting the programme. At around the same time, a number of factories around Northamptonshire began constructing trenches around or near to their premises. These, along the same lines as those dug around the racecourse, were to be used as shelter against bombing. In Higham Ferrers, people went one step further and gathered to build communal trenches in fields behind the High Street. All horse racing was temporarily suspended, and steel helmets arrived in the county for distribution to all air raid wardens. By mid-September, America had announced its intention to remain neutral and petrol rationing had begun. Across the county, petrol was priced at 1s. and 6d. (around 7p) a gallon. An agreement had been reached with fuel distributors whereby they would pool their resources. This meant that once supplies sold by brand name had been exhausted, they would be replaced by a single grade of petrol to be named 'Pool Motor Spirit'. No other grade or brand could then be sold for the duration of the war.

The Ministry of Food had been reformed and organized the setting up of Food Control Committees. In Northamptonshire they operated across the county, much as they had toward the end of 1918. Ration books had been printed back in 1938 in preparation for war, and the food committees were responsible for monitoring food distribution across the county. Their brief was to be responsible for five key areas:

➢ Registration of all consumers and the issue of rationing books/documents.

- Registration and licensing of all county retail dealers in foodstuffs.
- Certification of retailers' requirements as directed by the Ministry of Food.
- The transference of any registered customer from one retailer to another if there was just cause.
- Certification of the food requirements of hostels, residential and catering establishments, hotels and any other institutions agreed by the Ministry of Food.

So efficient had the government been that ration books had begun being issued to households by 8 September, though were not actually in use until the start of 1940. While the implementation of rationing had always been seen as an essential in the event of a war, there was initially a great deal of resistance to it. Yet when the country imported around 70 per cent of its food, including some 50 per cent of its meat, then there was an inevitability about it, because it was believed that merchant shipping would be attacked and import levels would fall as a consequence. It would prove to be an accurate assessment. At this early stage of the war, food was still in plentiful supply. Only sugar and potatoes had been brought under government control, their retail prices fixed at around 3d/lb and 1d/lb respectively, so there had been no panic buying or food hoarding.

On 11 September, Northamptonshire also formed a County War Executive Committee. This consisted of nine district sub-committees, which covered the following areas: Brackley, Brixworth, Daventry, Kettering, Northampton, Oundle, Thrapston, Towcester and Wellingborough. Each committee had seven members. The brief issued to the groups was to pull together the farming community across the county and reach agreements with every farmer concerning land most suitable for ploughing. The government had agreed that up until 31 December 1939, all land that had been under grass for not less than seven years would be eligible for a £2 per acre grant, but to receive the money it had to be ploughed and sown with an arable crop for harvest in 1940. The hope was that some 30,000 acres across Northamptonshire would be secured.

By the end of the same month, the National Registration Bill had been brought onto the statute books and implemented on 29 September. As no census had been carried out since 1931, it was essential for government to know exactly what manpower was available. Since the start of mobilization (conscription) and evacuation, there had obviously been a significant population shift. What was needed was information regarding every individual to facilitate the creation of maximum efficiency in what would become a war economy, and also to aid in assessing the effectiveness of food rationing. The information gathered was pretty straightforward:

Residence

Name

Sex

D.O.B.

Marital status

Occupation

If a member of armed forces or reserves

This allowed for future planning, both in the armed services and also in the workforce, and how it was spread geographically across the country.

As this information was being gathered, news was spreading that the British Expeditionary Force (BEF) had landed in France under the command of Lord Gort. The force itself consisted of some 150,000 men, 24,000 vehicles and all necessary supplies of fuel, ammunition and food. Initial reports told of no contact with German forces, which was probably to have been expected. The German army had not at this stage made any forward moves into Belgium or France. Elsewhere, though, the news was not so benign. German U-boats had sunk the British liner *Athenia*. Bound for Canada from Liverpool, she had been mistaken for a Royal Navy cruiser and sunk in the eastern Atlantic. All 112 on board had drowned. The Royal Navy had also lost aircraft carrier HMS *Courageous*, along with 500 of her crew, torpedoed off the coast of Ireland. Any thoughts that this war would be slow to impact were being quickly dispelled.

So too were any thoughts about aerial bombardment not being a feature of modern warfare. Reports filtering through during October were of the first air raid on Britain at Rosyth, Scotland, when German bombers attacked the Royal Navy base there. It was reported locally as an attack on the Forth Bridge, which was understandable, but erroneous. What we know now, but was not reported at the time, was that nine German bombers took part in the raid, and no air raid warning was sounded. They were fought off by Spitfires from Edinburgh and Glasgow, but only after they had inflicted damage on a number of Royal Navy ships, killing sixteen crew and wounding forty-four. But the news got worse. Reported at around the same time was the loss of HMS *Royal Oak*. Anchored in what was considered the impregnable Scapa Flow in the Orkneys, the ship was torpedoed and sunk, killing more than 800 sailors. It was a real body blow to British morale.

Not that people had time to reflect on the disaster. As winter began to set in and the blackout became a part of daily life, more attention was focused on maintaining total darkness. The raid on Scotland highlighted just how vulnerable towns and cities could be to German bombers if all lights were not extinguished on the long winter nights. To that end, it was realized that more work needed to be done, not only to ensure a true blackout, but also to minimize the

Soldiers of the BEF relaxing somewhere in France.

risk of accident to people moving around the streets at night. Torches had become the chosen light source for many, but even torchlight created a risk. It was therefore decided to paint white lines down the centre of paved areas through the towns and other built-up areas, the idea being that pedestrians would be directed to keep left and hopefully not feel the need to light their way. Kettering adopted the plan in November, and others followed. Northampton also created the Northampton Messengers, volunteers who, in the event of telephone lines being cut, whether through bombing or sabotage, would carry messages across the county by whatever means they had at their disposal. This generally meant by bicycle or motor bike, and the idea spread quickly, with messengers set up all across the county, although it is not clear how much use was ever made of them.

As Christmas approached, families sought out as much news as they could from the front line in Europe. The 2nd Battalion Northamptonshire Regiment had joined the BEF in October, so there was a keen interest for many in exactly what was happening across the Channel. But it was the Royal Navy who dominated headlines after reports in local newspapers of a sea battle off the coast of Argentina, which became known as the Battle of the River Plate. Three Royal Navy cruisers, HMS *Exeter*, *Ajax* and *Achilles* had fought a running battle with the German pocket battleship, *Admiral Graf Spee*. We know more about this battle today than people did back in 1939, particularly after it was made into a film in 1956, but just after the outbreak of war and after a number of naval setbacks, this was a morale-boosting victory that grabbed headlines all across the world, mainly due to the fact that the *Graf Spee*'s captain, Hans Langsdorff, had been forced to seek shelter in Montevideo after his ship had suffered significant damage in clashes with the British task force. Being a neutral port, the German ship was only allowed 72 hours in Montevideo for repairs, and then ordered to leave. Believing the British ships had been reinforced, Langsdorff decided to scuttle his ship rather than fight his way out of Argentinian waters. Perhaps the tragedy of this decision was his suicide three days later.

But on the Home Front the loss of the *Graf Spee* was something to celebrate as the year drew to a close. It was much needed; 1939 had been an eventful year, but in many ways the war was yet to come.

CHAPTER TWO

1940

Britain at Bay

Christmas had been a quiet time for many in Northamptonshire. The 'Phoney war', as it was being termed, had been a part of life for four months. Yet there had been no serious shortages, food prices had generally held up well, day-to-day business had continued comparatively unaffected and there had been no sign of an air attack. After the sudden shopping frenzy in early winter 1939, when people had clamoured to buy blinds, curtains, brown paper, cardboard and anything else that would help ensure their home infringed no blackout laws, things settled into a familiar routine. Determined not to allow Christmas to become a bleak affair, most had bought wisely but well, and so the season had been celebrated despite the threat of war, though without the ringing of church bells and perhaps the usual party noise.

January 1940 brought with it a sharp drop in temperatures, heralding one of the coldest winters on record but little news as to the state of affairs in Europe. At a local level, cinemas did a roaring trade during the dark nights, with John Wayne's *Stagecoach* proving popular, whilst in Kettering, *Cinderella* dominated at the Savoy. Earls Barton lost its siren after police had it removed on the grounds that it was unnecessary, and Rotary clubs were raising money to send chocolate out to the troops. With news from the front in short supply, local and national newspapers were carrying the story of Unity Mitford.

The Mitfords were well known, having attracted press interest since the mid 1930s. Unity, the fifth of seven children, along with sister Diana, had by this time attained significant notoriety due to their belief in the Nazi doctrine. Hence the huge press interest in them. Both were well known in Germany and counted Hitler as a friend. Diana eventually married Oswald Mosley, head of the British Union of Fascists, a man extremely familiar to most households through his activities in the East End of London and the formation of his Blackshirts. Their hatred of all things Jewish caused riots and streets fights, until they had been broken up in early 1937 after the government had introduced the Public Order Act, which banned the wearing of political or military style uniforms. Mosley also numbered among his group a man who would become even more reviled, William Joyce, otherwise known to any who listened to the radio in Northamptonshire throughout the war years as 'Lord Haw Haw'. Broadcasting from Berlin, where he had fled in the late summer of 1939, he was associated with his by now very familiar introduction to every broadcast: 'Germany calling, Germany calling, Germany calling.'

The Mitford sisters, both socialites, had been moving amongst some unsavoury characters for a number of years. Unity was obsessed with Hitler since her first meeting with him in 1935, and he in turn accepted her into his inner circle. It was a much-vaunted position in Germany and one she used well, Hitler allowing her to share a balcony with him in Vienna after the annexation of Austria, where he introduced her to the coterie of senior Nazi officers that surrounded him. This acceptance gave her a degree of influence which she exercised from time to time, attending rallies, giving speeches and eventually allowing the publication of one particularly unpleasant, anti-Jewish rant by the German newspaper *Der Stürmer*. The story inevitably found its way into the British national press and onto the breakfast tables of people across Britain. More importantly perhaps, it reinforced the view of many that she and her sister were collaborating with what had become the enemy.

It came as no surprise, then, when newspapers carried the story of her mysterious disappearance from Germany at the end of 1939 and her reappearance in southern England in the first few days of January 1940. Information was sketchy, but throughout the first week of the new year it was her story that dominated headlines and was discussed around the dinner tables, even more so as people discovered that she had apparently shot herself in the head in a failed suicide attempt. Her arrival back in England was described as a medical case, with speculation as to the how and why debated in both local and national press. Not that they were to uncover any salient facts. But they did expect, regardless of any gunshot wound, that she would be arrested and charged over her involvement with the Nazis. When she was not, it caused a degree of dismay. But like most news stories over the weeks that followed, it faded from the headlines, and whether or not Unity Mitford ever recovered became an irrelevance. We know today that she did survive, never faced any charges and died in 1948 a free woman, unlike sister Diana, who along with Mosley was interned in May 1940 and eventually imprisoned in Holloway.

It is doubtful this would have mattered to most people living across Northamptonshire. There were far more serious worries at home that began to overshadow those about the Mitfords' cheerless, dolorous lives. Rationing began on 8 January for butter, bacon and sugar, which made life for some uncomfortable at best. At sea, German mines had sunk the British liner the *Dunbar Castle* off the south coast, and news was breaking of German bombers having attacked Newcastle. The threat of aerial attack was getting ever closer. To counter this threat, it was decided to mount a county-wide check on all air raid sirens. Rather than waiting until an attack to discover there were problems, it was decided to sound the air raid siren alarm on every second Saturday of the month, at least in the short term. So across the county, from 11 January, the exercise was launched. It was probably a wise precaution at this stage of the war. Being so far inland, it was presumed German aircraft would be unable to penetrate this far, but if the German army made significant inroads across Europe, then Northamptonshire could be vulnerable. By mid-January, that scenario was beginning to raise its head as news filtered through of German soldiers massing on the North Sea island of Borkum in preparation of an attack on Holland, although news regarding British troops, including the Northamptonshire Regiment, stationed in northern France suggested the opposite was taking place along their front lines. It truly was a 'Phoney War'.

But winter was setting in both here and abroad. Appeals were made by the Red Cross for winter clothing to be sent on to the troops, and people all over the shire were doing what they could to help. Provided with wool by the Red Cross, the Women's Voluntary Service was organizing knitting groups, as were various industries whose staff came together to volunteer their time. Collectively they were producing socks, woollen hats, mittens, gloves, scarves, pullovers and blankets, all of which were gathered up at county centres and then sent on to the troops. Just as in the First World War, clubs and pubs were organizing raffles, dances, games and charitable collections, and local Rotary Clubs made financial donations to match or supplement any amounts raised to buy either luxuries or essentials. They were going to need it. Winter in Northamptonshire began closing in by mid-January, with temperatures plummeting below freezing.

The freeze brought the canal system across the county to a standstill. Some 1,500 barges were frozen in and over 50,000 tons of merchandise stopped in transit. Huge ice-breakers were brought in to try to free up as much traffic as possible, but in places they too were brought to a standstill. All across the county, anyone living on the water found themselves trapped by ice, children unable to attend school and travel at times brought to a standstill. By the last week of January, heavy snow had brought more chaos to all parts of Northamptonshire. Wollaston was entirely cut off, buses were abandoned around Kettering and traffic generally was unable to move because of the depth of the snow. When the snow melted, the inevitable flooding followed on, with criticism then levelled at the county council for its failure to clear roads and footpaths. What was not expected was the illness epidemic that swept across the county as the bad weather began to recede. Influenza, chills, bronchitis, German measles, tonsillitis and heavy colds impacted severely on all industries. Many older people died as a result. Those working in the shoe industry, retail and steel manufacture were hard hit, with a number of employers resorting to providing their staff with daily doses of an influenza mixture in an attempt to keep the germs at bay and production at required levels. In Corby, it was thought the abnormal atmospheric conditions had increased pollution levels. Emissions of dust and grit from the steel furnaces were unable to escape and disperse at high enough levels. This meant it simply swept over the town, settling on homes, roads, cars and, of course, people. In turn it had, in places, buried the lying snow in a thick grey blanket, and after being breathed in by workers travelling to and from home or those out shopping, had caused nose and throat irritations. Doctors reported being unable to cope and hospitals were understaffed after nurses fell ill. All in all, January was a month to forget.

Not that February 1940 started any better. The aftermath of all this atrocious weather and the medical consequences took a week or two to settle down. When it had, a debate began across the county as to whether or not to build shelters in the various towns or whether it would be better to simply line existing trench systems with concrete and use them as an alternative. The Anderson shelter construction plans were already under way. At this stage it was about how to protect people in areas where they tended to congregate, whether through work, leisure or shopping. Kettering had proposed public shelters on its high street that could accommodate around thirty people, and Northampton and Wellingborough were looking at the same sort of idea. Others were examining the various terraced streets where Andersons would not work because of the lack of garden space. A proposal here was to build shelters in the centre of the street. These were debates that would go on throughout the year.

But it was not only shelters that were needed. A report presented to Northamptonshire's Education Committee at around the same time had identified around 10 per cent of elementary school children as being under-nourished. With war already impacting on diet through the rationing system, it was feared those on low incomes, many of whom were already struggling, would find it difficult to improve their children's diet whilst restrictions existed. In order to help these families it was proposed to begin supplying their children with free milk. According to the committee, it would cost the council around £750 a year, and the government – who had already been informed of this situation developing across the whole country – had agreed a subsidy of around 50 per cent. The council readily agreed to act, but only if supplies were distributed to those where earnings, after paying rent, equated to less than 7s per head per week (around 35p today) and had been identified as in need by the School Medical Officer. As time went by, of course, this evolved into provision for all children of this age, but that was some way off at this stage. Nevertheless, it was a key decision at a very difficult time, as was that to ration coal. Fortunately, the atrocious winter weather was on its way out when coal rationing was announced, although temperatures were still hovering around freezing. Supplies throughout the first couple of months of the year had been irregular, so much so that across Corby many homes had resorted to breaking up furniture for the fire to keep warm. It was no surprise to many then when it was announced that only 2cwt (101.6kg) of coal per fortnight was to be allowed for each household. In turn, costs were pushed up by the extra bagging required to meet the restriction, reaching around 2s 9d (14p) a cwt by the end of March.

At about the same time as this was being decided, the County Master Butchers Association was meeting in Northampton. Fear of a reduction in meat supplies reaching Britain caused by German submarine activity had prompted the government to plan to introduce meat rationing in March 1940. The association had come together to argue the merits for and against the scheme, and try to plan how to implement it across the county. It is fair to say they were not happy with the meat allocation allowed under the scheme, arguing the amount each family was to be allowed would prove inadequate.

Meat rationing – unlike sugar, butter and bacon – was to be based on cost, not weight. Each adult was to be allowed to purchase meat to the value of 1s. and 2d. (6p) each week. To the meat trade, that meant households would only be able to buy poorest

Advert informing households to register for their meat ration.

cuts or sausages, which were not rationed at this stage but of poor quality. As was pointed out at the Northampton meeting, 'with mutton chops at 1s 10d a lb [9p], and rump steaks at 2s 2d [11p] the whole of the rations of the man and wife will be gone in a couple of days.' For butchers who worked on a 20 per cent margin, this would inevitably cause issues because the sales of higher-value meat would simply disappear. In turn, the fear was that it would cause a number of butchers to shut up shop and walk away. For the industry, this idea of rationing on price was clearly problematical. The government, though, was not about to change its strategy, and the Butchers Association knew it. What they were really attempting to do, apart from argue their case, was find a solution to a problem that was likely to last as long as the war did. It actually lasted much longer, and as the war continued they and their group became extremely adept at supplying meat to households. Housewives were equally adept at changing the family diet to accommodate, helped no doubt by a series of cookery demonstrations set up by the Electricity Supply Authority in their showrooms around the county. The purpose was to teach housewives how to cook more nutritious foods whilst living on a limited diet. Keen to promote the idea that good quality meals could still be produced with fewer, or different ingredients, local and national newspapers began publishing a variety of new recipes. Radio broadcasting schedules were also changed in order that new programmes could be created to advise people on what foods they ought to be buying, how these should be prepared and the types of nutritious meals they could make. It was successful in the main, because a great deal of thought and planning by government had taken place prior to the war to assess the effects of rationing. From these early discussions and secret trials, the government had deduced that the reduction and changes in diet would prove more positive than had originally been believed. They were right, but living with these restrictions – and more foods were to be added to the list as time went by – was certainly not easy.

    March also saw the election of John Profumo (who had spoken at Rothwell in 1939 and many years later would be involved in the Christine Keeler scandal) as the Conservative MP for Kettering. After a long and, at times, bitter by-election, he had defeated an anti-war candidate by a majority of over 6,000. In the Army by this time, Profumo entered the Houses of Parliament as the youngest MP to have been elected. He was well respected by those who knew him and equally, at this stage of his career, by the people in and around Kettering.

News coming back from France was still very sketchy. The only reported contact with German forces involved the Northamptonshire Regiment somewhere along the Maginot Line. According to local newspapers, a patrol had entered a cottage known to have been occupied by German troops. No German soldiers were found, though there apparently were signs of occupation and they did discover a German gramophone along with twenty-two records and a radio. The soldiers carried the gramophone back to their own lines. On the following night they returned for the radio but found it had gone. The gramophone would be returned to England and placed in the unit's museum. Other than that, all was still quiet.

Everyone knew it couldn't last. To that end, over the last few months a number of independent and reasonably successful

Northampton Town and County Hall.

attempts to raise money for the war had been ongoing, in part to enable the purchase of goods for those soldiers serving abroad and in part to assist the overall war effort. But it had been realized that what was needed was a more co-ordinated effort; some way of pulling all these charitable events together under a central committee that could better manage their success or failure. At a crowded meeting held in Northampton's County Council Chamber, addressed by Northampton's Mayor, Alderman Glenn, it was agreed that wherever possible, all future charitable events would be centrally controlled by a committee consisting of members of the Red Cross, St John Ambulance and a few other voluntary associations that were still to be decided. In many ways it made sense, as since the start of the war around £5,000 had already been raised across the county. This sum, it was argued, could probably be substantially increased if organized events became common across the whole of Northamptonshire. To facilitate this, it was agreed one of the key charity events for 1940 would be the organizing of Flag Days. Four dates were agreed – 18 May, 29 June, 10 August and 7 September. These events aimed to raise in excess of £10,000 and to support not just the Red Cross and St John Ambulance, but also the RNLI, the British Soldiers Society and the Mission to Seamen, everyone being all too well aware that at this stage of the war the naval services had borne the brunt.

That changed somewhat during the early part of April, when newspapers began reporting that the Germans had launched an invasion of Denmark and Norway. Denmark quickly capitulated; Norway did not. Resistance there was fierce, and Britain and France moved to support the Norwegians by organizing a joint force that landed in central Norway on 14 April. The war had suddenly escalated, and not where it had been expected. Britain now had troops on two fronts, and it was being reported that the RAF was mounting a series of bombing raids into Scandinavia. There was growing concern in Northamptonshire and across the country that an attack on France was now inevitable.

But life here went on as normal. The government announced an increase in rail fares, much to everyone's disgust. The cost of a monthly return from Northampton to London increased from 11s. 7d. (58p) to 12s. 9d. (64p). The Cobblers (Northampton Town) beat Watford 2-1 in the Football League Cup, and the government health minister, Walter Elliot, arrived in Northampton to begin a tour of the county. The purpose of his visit – which began after a lengthy meeting with the heads of the ARP, ambulance service, education and health and various sections of the medical service – was to assess the viability of the county should casualties arising from air attacks prove heavier than anticipated. By the end of the month, with information coming in from Norway still sketchy, attention was switching to the radio and the first war budget. Chancellor of the Exchequer Sir John Simon obviously needed to raise more revenue, and announced expected increases on the usual list of revenue drivers:

    beer up 1d a pint;

    whisky up 1s 9d a bottle;

    tobacco up 3d an ounce;

    cigarettes up 1d on a pack of ten retailed at 5d;

    matches up ½d from 1d.

To make matters worse, he also reduced the married man's personal allowance from £180 per year to £170 per year. Clearly the war was going to hit everyone in the pocket, whether they supported it or not. On the good news front, Joe Loss and his band opened at the Regal in Kettering, Leslie Howard and Ingrid Bergman were playing at the Exchange cinema in Northampton and the price of a Bush radio had fallen to just over £11.

    Entertainment in all its guises was critically important for morale across the whole of the county, even more so at the start of May 1940. Out in Norway, newspapers and radio broadcasts were beginning to indicate that all was not well. British forces were withdrawing from Trondheim. On a local level, the ARP had launched the most ambitious, thought-provoking civil defence exercise it had ever undertaken. Planned in secret, it was a comprehensive mobilization test carried out across the county. Its intention was to test the emergency services, industry and the reaction of people who would be affected were it a real-life situation. In conjunction with Lincolnshire, Derbyshire, Nottinghamshire and Leicestershire, the plan presumed that three towns, their identity kept secret until the morning of the exercise, were being heavily bombed. The supposed attack was being carried out by 100 enemy bombers, dropping some 1,400 bombs in total, responsible for over 1,200 deaths and 2,700 injured across the chosen regions.

At 7 am on 5 May, all areas received a 'yellow' warning that enemy bombers had been sighted crossing the coast. RAF fighters were shown as being scrambled, and at 9.30 am Northampton's warning turned 'red', a clear indicator they were one of the chosen targets. Within twenty minutes, full mobilization of all the town's emergency services had been achieved. According to the brief they were given that morning, seventeen areas across the town had been hit by enemy bombers. These included Northampton General Hospital, which in turn put Kettering Hospital and Wellingborough Hospital on alert and caused soldiers to rush to the bomb-ravaged hospital wing to protect it from crowds. Abington Square was devastated and the town's main sewer and water supply blown up, Weston Place, Adnitt Place, Weston Street and York Place all badly bombed, and Mulliners on Bridge Street was blown up. Fire engines were despatched all across town, decontamination squads attended supposed gas attacks and water engineers were called out to all sites involving water loss. Volunteers played the part of casualties, and there were many of them, and as the exercise came to a close at 12.30 pm – with the presumed loss of life around 105 and the injured around 300 – it was rightly deemed a huge success. The response time to any supposedly affected area had been eight minutes, which was not only a great achievement but also incredibly reassuring. Every area of the civil defence team under the ARP banner had proved its worth. The hope, of course, was that they would never be needed.

Five days later, Hitler's armies attacked Holland, Belgium and Luxembourg. The Luftwaffe began to bomb RAF bases across France, and the British were in retreat in Norway. Chamberlain lost the confidence of the House of Commons and resigned, Winston Churchill replacing him as the new Prime Minister. The 'Phoney War' was at an end, and so were the exercises; from this point on, it was going to be very much for real. Any who doubted the government's intention to prosecute the war to its conclusion had to reassess after it announced compulsory conscription for those aged between 19 and 36. As if to emphasize the point, British troops also landed in Iceland to prevent any attempt at German occupation, which would have given Hitler greater control over shipping in the North Atlantic. By 15 May, Holland had fallen, meaning, at a local level, that the shoe industry had lost one of its key customers.

Things were suddenly moving fast. The German armies' rapid advance across the Netherlands, the fall of Luxembourg at the end of the French Maginot Line, the imminent collapse of neutral Belgium and the anticipated attack against France all racked up the tension. Listening to the radio suddenly became a national obsession. Unlike the First World War, people now had access to faster, often more accurate news. The BBC, despite censorship, was able to report on events happening across the Channel much faster than the press could, and speed was of the essence, though at this stage of the German offensive, information broadcast was not necessarily veracious. The war front was wide and the fighting intense. Nevertheless, for those gathered around their wireless sets at home, it quickly became obvious that this was not going to be a static war. There would be no long lines of trenches this time, where thousands hurled themselves across no man's land to gain a patch of mud. This was mechanized warfare, the type of which had never been seen before, where swift movement on the ground was matched by support from the air. It was something that it appeared the German armies were well capable of, and perhaps the BEF were not. Throughout May, the news coming out of France was calamitous.

It was in such circumstances that Anthony Eden, Secretary of State for War, broadcast an appeal for volunteers to form a Local Defence Volunteer Corps. The German army had used parachutists in certain sectors of the battle front, and they had proved themselves extremely effective, which led to a fear they could employ a similar tactic in any future attack on Britain. What was needed was a home-grown force that could police the country, guard important points, observe and report accurately, and defend villages, factories or other vital points in or around towns. They were also to be utilized in the setting-up of roadblocks to prevent easy, unchallenged movement around the country. Churchill would eventually call these men The Home Guard. Across Northamptonshire, queues of men between the ages of 17 and 65 began forming outside police stations within twenty-four hours.

Members of the Home Guard as they looked later in the war.

All that was needed to enrol were a few salient facts: nationality; occupation; military experience; firearm experience; membership of Civil Defence.

On the first day of enrolment, 100 had joined in Wellingborough by midday, and the number swelled to thousands across the county by the end of the day. The formation of a new fighting arm of the army had proved a huge success. According to Major-General Sir Hereward Wake, Commandant of Northamptonshire's volunteer force, the plan after enlistment was to create six divisions across the whole county, including the Soke of Peterborough. Each town and village was to have at least forty men, all of whom, in time, would be in uniform and armed. Their role was to support the police, army and ARP for the duration of the war. Generally speaking, the idea worked well, with each division commanded by an experienced, retired military man and run on military lines.

But they would take time to train, and the fear of parachutists was seen as a very real and present threat. It was therefore decided that until they could be fully utilized, the eyes on the ground would initially be only local police and soldiers, who would have the unenviable task of restricting movement around the county. Wasting no time, random check points were quickly set up to verify identity documents, check loads and generally monitor activity across the

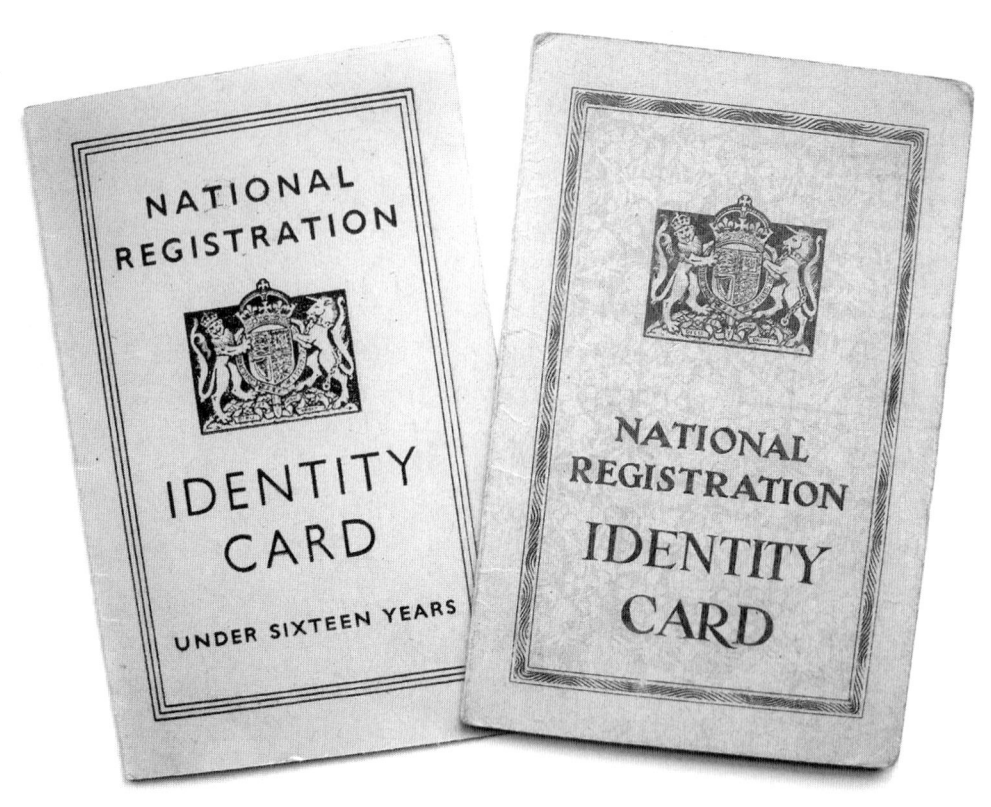

Identification cards were carried by everyone during the war.

county. Any driver or passenger who could not produce an identity card found their journey halted. Some were detained, many more simply turned around and sent back the way they had come. May 1940 and the months that followed established a precedent: no ID cards meant no travel. People adapted quickly, and in general supported the initiative, helped no doubt by advertised warnings in both newspapers and cinemas about the constant threat from Hitler's Germany. The scope of these threats obviously changed as the war progressed, but in this early stage, the fear of attacks from formations of Junkers aircraft, each carrying twenty parachutists, was very real. Meanwhile, the BEF was falling back in the face of the German advance and beginning to focus on the small coastal town of Dunkirk.

On 28 May, news broke that the Belgian army had surrendered. At the same time, British troops were already boarding ships to return home. Churchill had taken the decision that France would not survive the Germans' lightning advance, and plans were put into action to withdraw the BEF. Paris was in shock. German air superiority, rapid movement by ground forces and the breakout in the Ardennes had caused confusion and near collapse of the Anglo-French armies in the north of the country. All that was known at home was that a rearguard action was being fought by the British and French around the coast, allowing the British to withdraw. Here at home, as people began to understand the tragedy taking place across the Channel, attention turned toward the fate of the Northamptonshires. The 2nd and 5th Battalions were in France and heavily involved in the fighting retreat; the 2nd around Arras and the Ypres-Comines Canal, the 5th around the River Escaut. Both battles would have an impact on a number of families across the county. It was not known back home at the time, of course, but casualties had been extremely heavy, with both battalions severely reduced in number in the retreat to the French coast and the ships waiting off the beaches at Dunkirk; many, as we now know, were small ships, some of which had never left the River Thames before. They, and the Royal Navy, were responsible for extracting some 338,000 Allied soldiers from the beaches, including some 113,000 Frenchmen. A further 160,000 or so were later evacuated from Boulogne, Le Havre, Cherbourg, St Nazaire and Bourdeaux. There is no doubting the success of this venture, despite the fact it was a retreat and defeat. Without the bravery of the Royal Navy, those small boats and the RAF, it would have been a far greater disaster than it was.

For some, though, it seemed an irrelevance. In Leicester, the Conscientious Objectors Court sat to hear cases from across Northamptonshire. Men attended from Kettering, Desborough, Rushden, Rothwell, Woodford, Burton Latimer and Northampton, most intent on refusing military service in whatever guise, others more than happy to serve but only in a medical capacity. In the case of the latter, the court quickly accepted them for non-combative service. For the rest, it was far more difficult. At the outbreak of war, public opinion had been relatively indifferent. At this stage, with heavy fighting and losses in France, that was no longer the case. People's attitudes had begun to harden. Questions were raised as to why an individual should expect to be allowed to withdraw from the military – unless they were deeply, and provably, religious – particularly at a time of real crisis when the country looked to be under threat of invasion. In some industries, in fact, this had already led to workers refusing to work with those known to be objectors. In other industries, objectors had lost their jobs and were ostracized from the neighbourhood in which they lived. At the court in Leicester, a fair number of these men found themselves in awkward, problematical situations when questioned by a panel of independent tribunal members, especially when unable to explain their reasoning, often religion-based, due to a lack of religious knowledge. That's not to say every case floundered. Some were accepted by the court due to straitened circumstances within a family, where forced enlistment would have been both unfair and detrimental to the family left at home. Each case was heard and fairly judged on its individual merits.

Elsewhere in the county, Borough Engineers were working under considerable pressure to keep up the delivery and erection of air raid shelters. The government had been forced to pull the plug on supplying Anderson shelters. What had been delivered to Northamptonshire by the end of May was all that was now going to arrive. Steel, it had been decided, was likely to be in greater demand for the war effort, particularly in munitions, than for building shelters. Alternatives would have to be found. Brick and concrete had been trialled and were now proposed as 'domestic communal' shelters, essentially because they were intended to house up to forty-eight people at any one time and could be erected quickly on any piece of spare land adjacent to housing. At Northampton's County Ground, the Empire Day Parade had taken place before the Mayor and hundreds of cheering spectators, involving around 1,000 young people drawn from the Boys' Brigade, Girls' Friendly Society, Boy Scouts, Girls' Life Brigade and St John Ambulance Cadets. It had proved a welcome distraction from the war news. Most organizations embraced the council's decision not to cancel the event in the face of objections from the Girl Guides, who were refused permission to participate by their headquarters due to the war. Elsewhere, the Cobblers lost 7-2 to Sheffield Wednesday and on the last Sunday in May, the king called for a National Day of Prayer, which was well-supported by most families and reflected in the size of congregations that packed out churches across the county.

By the start of June, some 2,300 men had formed queues outside the county's various Labour Exchanges to enlist in the armed forces. The criterion for acceptance was simply that all applicants be born between 1 January 1912 and 25 May 1920. They would form part of the first draft of recruits from across the country and would begin to fill the gaps left after Dunkirk, a key policy after Churchill told the Commons that 30,000 men of the BEF had either been killed, wounded or were missing, while around 1,000 pieces of artillery and armoured transport had been lost. This was a clear indicator of just how serious home defence had become.

As if to emphasize the point, it was reported nationally that small numbers of German bombers had begun to attack the south and south-east of Britain. Then, on 10 June, Mussolini finally brought Italy into the war, his forces joining Hitler in the battle for France. The outlook was bleak, but not desperate. Canadian forces had been arriving in Britain since the start of the year. Northampton welcomed them with cheering crowds at the beginning of June as they arrived at East Park Parade. Those who returned from France with the BEF were back in training and slowly being re-armed. The RAF was intact, despite its losses over France, and food supplies, though rationed, were not under severe pressure. In many ways it was a breathing space, a pause, time to restructure and reorganize. Everyone was all too well aware of what was coming once Hitler had completed his European conquest, although the war across the Channel was still going on in early June.

Little actually changed through the rest of the month, despite the fall of France and the signing of an armistice by the French Government on 21 June. In Northamptonshire, home life continued pretty much as it had throughout the first half of the year. The ARP continued its recruitment drive across the county for more volunteers. Cinemas continued their protests over Sunday closure, which had been ongoing since war was declared. The 'Dig for Victory' campaign was in full swing, with locally based troops helping dig over land for food planting. Kettering and Wellingborough councils agreeing to release more council land for use as allotments. Railings were cut down and taken away for scrap, households gave up their aluminium saucepans to help build aeroplanes and people donated money to a variety of wartime causes.

The event that caused the greatest amount of publicity in Northamptonshire at the start of the summer, though, was

Northampton County Council's decision to sack all conscientious objectors. Since the hearings in Leicester – and by this time there had been more than one – the realization that Britain was now under siege caused a significant hardening of public opinion. This prompted a two-hour council meeting, at times heated, at which it was decided by a huge majority that all conscientious objectors in the employ of the council be sacked. Reinstatement for the duration of the war would then follow, if they wished, but at the same rate of pay as they would have received as a serving soldier. For many, this would mean a reduction in salary. The decision, strongly supported by the county branch of NALGO (National Association of Local Government Officers) and the majority of councillors, was implemented immediately. The strongest argument in support of the motion was the belief held by most that if the country was not worth defending, it was not worth living in. Opposition from the Society of Friends (Quakers) was heard, but carried little weight. Clearly there was considerable anger about conscientious objectors, although it was not aimed at all. For most people, that anger was reserved for those who refused to take any part in the defence of the nation, yet expected to remain in peacetime employment, particularly when wives, mothers and dependents were likely to find themselves struggling on service pay and allowances, and possibly even become impoverished, if the key wage-earner was subsequently killed or maimed on active service. It was an emotive and divisive issue.

On a lighter note, in an attempt to deflect concerns about the war, rationing and food prices, but raise the profile of the importance of salvage (recycling), all evacuee children were invited to submit works for a public exhibition. There were no restrictions on what the children could do, only that it must have some artistic merit and be created from waste materials. Hundreds of exhibits were on show during July, demonstrating various levels of skill and all created from a variety of discarded products, including old wallpaper, bottles, bits of cardboard, newspapers and fabric off-cuts. Helped by their foster parents and teachers the children's exhibits ranged from sculptures using old tin cans to objects made from wine corks, dress-making, millinery, bookbinding, paintings and various designs made from bits of old wood and glue. The exhibition was a huge success in bringing these children together and allowing them to express themselves in whatever medium they chose, and was certainly well attended by a public keen to help them settle into what were really their second homes.

But the war was never far away. The first phase of the Battle of Britain for control of the skies over the country so that a cross-Channel invasion could follow had begun around the start of July. Across Northamptonshire, there was little sign of any of this due to the fact that all the attacks at this stage were directed at shipping in the Channel and on our coastal ports. The German plan was to draw the RAF out and weaken it significantly in combat with Luftwaffe fighters, a plan that failed because Britain had radar, which allowed the RAF to target the bombers and, wherever possible, avoid the fighters. The tactic resulted in ever increasing losses for the Luftwaffe, which caused them to change their approach. So began the second phase. Unable to draw the RAF into the type of aerial combat they sought, the Luftwaffe instead attempted to destroy some of the British forward air bases, hit coastal ports harder, destroy radar and bomb other designated targets scattered across southern Britain. For some two weeks or so, groups of German bombers also began to move further inland, with Northamptonshire suffering its first air raid on 16 August when fourteen high-explosive bombs fell on Kilsby. Later that month, bombs fell at Duston, destroying one bungalow, partially destroying a second and bringing down electric cables and electrocuting the ARP warden who had rushed to help.

By the end of August, sustaining far heavier losses than anticipated, the Luftwaffe changed its direction of attack once again, launching phase three. With a need to minimize those losses, in both aircraft and flight crew, the Luftwaffe had taken the decision to only fly in mass bombing formations and aim every attack at the RAF's southern bases. Each attack consisted of around 100 or more bombers, all flying in a tight formation and escorted by large numbers of German fighters. The strategy was to inflict enough damage to the airfields that the Spitfires and Hurricanes would not be able to land, re-arm and refuel. History records that this was probably the nearest Hitler ever came to winning the air superiority he needed. According to most statistics, the RAF suffered the loss of around 450 aircraft in this phase of the battle, with 230 pilots killed or wounded. So effective was this strategy that by the beginning of September, Fighter Command's position was seriously compromised. But the leader of Germany's Luftwaffe, Hermann Göring, had not reckoned on Hitler.

Whilst the bombers had been attacking the British mainland, RAF Bomber Command had been hitting back along the French coast. On 24 August they had ventured even further afield and bombed Berlin for the first time. Hitler, enraged by their audacity, ordered Göring to change his tactics yet again and start to bomb London in retaliation. So began phase four of the Battle of Britain on 7 September, which provided the breathing space an embattled Fighter Command needed. Although the attacks on London wrought havoc and caused huge numbers of casualties, the losses suffered by German aircrew were appalling. Bombing in daylight hours in mass formations in one place gave the RAF the opportunity to inflict maximum damage, and they took it. So great was the destruction inflicted that by 1 October, the Luftwaffe began the fifth and final phase of the air campaign, to bomb southern England by day and London by night. By this time the tide had turned. The Luftwaffe was never going to achieve air superiority, and by the start of the second week in October Hitler had cancelled all invasion plans. The bombing of British towns and cities continued, but the Battle of Britain had been won by the RAF. The recorded losses made for sober reading. Britain lost some 915 aircraft, the Luftwaffe around 1,700, and the loss of life to both sides was large.

A German bomber somewhere over Britain.

There had also been further bombing across Northamptonshire. Pury End at Paulerspury was hit by two land mines; these were 8ft-long cylinders dropped by parachute. The blast damaged some fifty houses, but luckily there were no fatalities. At Rushden, people were not so lucky. The town was hit on 3 October when Alfred Street School was bombed, killing seven children and four adults and badly injuring forty others. The Victoria Hotel and several shops and houses were also damaged. War was beginning to bite hard.

There were also a number of German spies, one of whom landed by parachute outside the village of Denton, some 6 miles from Northampton. In early September 1940, local farmer Cliff Beechener, a member of the by now renamed Home Guard, was roused from his bed in the early morning by one of his farm labourers. In a nearby field, he claimed to have seen a man clutching a suitcase, sleeping in a dry ditch. Curious, and armed with a shotgun, the farmer followed the labourer's directions. What he found was a middle-aged man, wearing horn-rimmed spectacles, holding a leather case and sleeping on a parachute. When the man – who we now know was called Gosta Caroli – awoke and saw the gun, he stood up, surrendered and told the farmer he was Swedish and had travelled from Hamburg. The parachute was obviously a bit of a giveaway, and when the suitcase was opened it contained a wireless transmitter. There was no doubting the purpose of Caroli's mission. The farmer took him back to the farm house, and called his landlord, Lord Northampton, and the police. According to what was reported at the time, Caroli thought he had parachuted into Yardley, near Birmingham. He was carrying £200 in bank notes, an identity card with a Birmingham address, a revolver, maps and a bottle of brandy. The confusion no doubt lay with the pilot, who had dropped him near Yardley Hastings in error for the Birmingham drop zone. He was arrested later that day and handed over to MI5. MI5 had become expert at turning German agents into double agents, and Caroli was to become another. Over the next few months, he worked for them under the code name 'Summer', but after escaping and almost making it back to the coast, he was recaptured and placed in a prison camp near Oxford in 1941, where he remained for the remainder of the war. Had he made it back to France, the double-agent system would have been blown.

MI5 had clearly developed a successful and top secret strategy for dealing with German agents. This was not known until many years after the war, as information allowed into the public arena was carefully managed, for obvious reasons. But as the Battle of Britain raged in the skies above the country, the government decided the time was right to begin a morale-boosting programme of open air meetings under its banner of 'tell the people'. Officials organized tours across the counties in loudspeaker vans. In Northamptonshire, the van, with its accompanying staff, began in the market square at Rothwell, and over the course of several days visited Desborough, Kettering, Higham Ferrers, Thrapston, Rushden, Wellingborough, Brackley, Towcester and Daventry. At each stopping-off point, they would impart information about the war, its progress, air raids and how the necessary precautions worked, how Britain would thwart any German attack on the mainland and, most importantly, how Britain would eventually win. The tour proved hugely successful, drawing large crowds, enthusiastic applause and definitely helping to restore confidence wherever it went.

Confidence certainly needed a bit of a boost from time to time. Rushden was bombed a second time in November, killing four adults and one child, and on 15 November, 440 German bombers crossed the county en route to Coventry. Hundreds turned out to watch the horizon glow as more than 1,000 tons of high explosive hit the cathedral city. The number killed and seriously injured in the devastating raid numbered around 1,400. In Northamptonshire, some 300 incendiary bombs fell on Lowick at 3.30 am on 11 December. The following day, nine high explosive bombs fell on Islip, and on 12 December bombs fell around Geddington. In London, meanwhile, the Blitz had begun, and night-time bombing had for many become the norm.

Christmas 1940 was never going to be a raucous affair. Chocolates and sweets were already in short supply by this time. Meat was carefully rationed, as were clothes, tea, margarine and butter. All retail shops had been ordered to close at 6 pm every night, except for Friday and Saturday when they were allowed an extra hour. Thursday was a compulsory half-day closing, and blackout measures were rigidly enforced. Across the county, immunization against the spread of diphtheria had begun for all

Clearing up in Rushden after the October 1940 air raid (Northampton Central Library).

children. Meanwhile, all households were encouraged to take in soldiers to share their Christmas dinners. The year was ending for many on a sober note, with expectations of a better 1941 somewhat tempered by anxiety.

CHAPTER THREE

1941
Defeats and Setbacks

The New Year began with news of a victory. Since the Italians had entered the war, after a limited involvement in France, their main effort had been in North Africa. The fall of France in June 1940 had automatically neutralized the French forces in North Africa, along with Lebanon and Syria. This gave Mussolini's desert army of 250,000 men an unforeseen opportunity to fill the vacuum and chase the British forces out of Egypt. After the war on the Western Front had reached its conclusion, and whilst Hitler's bombers were blitzing Britain, Mussolini had seized that opportunity and launched an attack from Libya, initially making a successful advance as far as the port of Sidi Barrani, where the Italians were forced to pause when their supplies ran out. Then, possibly feeling secure in the belief that he could not now fail to achieve his overall objective, Mussolini ordered the invasion of Greece. This meant the remaining Italians in the desert, whose numbers were reduced as a consequence, would be forced onto the defensive, which suddenly made them vulnerable. Recognizing this, British forces under General Sir Archibald Wavell attacked the Italians throughout December and won a stunning victory, taking over 100,000 prisoners and forcing the Italian army to retreat. So there was good news at last for the people at home, and though they were not aware of it at the time, the Western Desert was one arena of war that was set to dominate newspaper headlines for the next two years.

On the Home Front, whilst this was welcome news, much was being made of the various schemes being set up to help raise money for the war effort, vital if the country was to withstand the German advance and reform, re-equip, re-arm and rebuild the armed

Italian soldiers captured after the British advance in North Africa.

services who had taken a battering on all fronts. The Red Cross Agricultural Fund had been set up to raise money that could be used to buy food, clothing and tobacco for prisoners of war, as well as providing some funding for convalescent homes, mobile X-ray units and financial relief for those made homeless after bombing attacks. Well supported, by mid-January it had raised some half a million pounds. A workman's fund had also been set up to help families of serving personnel. The YMCA was organizing garden sales, while the WVS (Women's Voluntary Service) was running supper dances, whist drives, bazaars, darts matches, charity concerts and other fundraising events. Knitting circles were set up across the county to produce gloves, hats and scarves, and there were more of the various flag days that had proved so successful in 1940. In short, anything that could raise money was put into place. By far the greatest success was in War Savings. Savings clubs were formed, some through a growing number of shops who ran savings schemes for their customers, others amongst street residents who formed their own savings groups (Northamptonshire had 150 of them in January 1940) or housewives who formed groups with friends, all supported by government-run marketing campaigns which operated throughout the war years. By the start of 1941, Northampton had already amassed over £1 million, and was pushing for another £500,000. Running alongside this were the week-long fundraising efforts that were organized across the county each year of the war – such as War Weapons Week and Buy a Spitfire Week – and proved equally successful.

Everyone, it seems, was committed to helping the war effort in some way. To that end, apart from these various savings schemes, there were a wide variety of local events designed to either simply raise more money or produce usable goods for the voluntary services. Geddington, for example, organized a supper dance of sausage and mash, with music from a local band. Held at the village hall, its intention was to support the Home Guard, ARP, Special Constables and the WVS. Across Wellingborough, volunteers organized money collections in pubs and clubs for the Workmen's Fund. Oundle people began donating blankets, clothing and socks, as well as money, whilst most villages across the north of the county ran hugely successful knitting circles, providing woollen garments for serving troops, all of which were collected each month and sent to the Red Cross Depot at Polebrook aerodrome. Supporting these efforts were the WI (Women's Institute), who organized mammoth jam-making sessions, the jam then sold on through retail outlets as part of the ration, with the proceeds added to the war chest. Northamptonshire created some 140 jam-making centres. Added to all this was the proceeds of jumble sales, church donations and dances in village halls across the county. This certainly had become a people's war.

Yet that war rolled on relentlessly, and with it came the growing potential for serious damage to homes from aerial attack. At this stage of the war, bombing had become a way of life around the country. People were growing accustomed to the news coming out of London and the big cities, where Luftwaffe raids had a significant effect. Fire-watching schemes were set up across the shire, involving householders banding together to form street fire-fighting groups in the more densely occupied places. Kettering, for example, had around eighty-five schemes in January 1941, essentially acting as extensions of the fire service. Provided with stirrup pumps, which they bought for £1, and sand – either bagged or in drums – they were expected to douse incendiary bombs where they could, or at least attempt to control smaller fires until fire engines could reach them. Alongside this initiative, fire-watching groups were formed, particularly in villages. Local councils organized deliveries of sand to villages all across Northamptonshire, and householders in rural areas were encouraged to take a bucketful home in order that they too could extinguish any small nearby fires, hopefully being alerted by those volunteering for fire-watching each night.

All of this was essential, not just for local homes but also for industry. Northamptonshire was growing in importance for the contribution its industries were beginning to make to the war effort. In the shoe industry, a huge amount of work had been done to try to develop footwear for airmen that would both insulate at low temperatures and also not jeopardize aircrew if they were shot down over enemy territory. It had transpired that it had proved impossible for the resistance movement in occupied countries to obtain spare civilian shoes, so when aircrew parachuted having been shot down over occupied territory, their tell-tale boots often led to their capture. The county's shoe industry successfully developed a boot that could be turned into a shoe. The escape boot, as it became known, had a knife inserted in a slit to one side of the sheepskin lining. This could then be used to cut away the boot leg, leaving a good quality Oxford shoe. It went into production late in 1940, and by 1941 between 80–100 pairs a week were being produced. The leg of the boot was eventually replaced with black suede, as leather shortages forced production changes.

The Express Lift Company, which had three factories at Harlestone Road and St John's Street Station, Northampton, and at Syston in Leicestershire, had begun manufacturing a wide variety of wartime products. Shells, aircraft instrument panels for Wellington bombers and bomb aimer panels were amongst some of their main work.

Wallis and Linnell Ltd made the service garments for the WAAF (Women's Auxiliary Air Force), WRNS (Women's Royal Naval Service), ATS (Auxiliary Territorial Service), Observer Corps and RAF. According to figures published after the war, they produced between 100,000 and 200,000 different garments from their Kettering factories.

Stewarts & Lloyd of Corby produced the steel tubes used in beach defences, which were later covered in barbed wire and utilized all across southern England. Known as Admiralty Scaffolding, it was deployed at all potential landing areas to prevent any invasion force gaining a foothold. One of its main advantages was its ability, when correctly placed, to prevent tanks forcing a beach landing. Later in the war, the company also produced the pipeline laid across the Channel known as 'Pluto' (Pipeline under the ocean) to provide petrol from the British coastline to Allied forces on the continent after D-Day.

Basset-Lowke Ltd in Northampton – essentially a toy company specializing in model railways, boats and ships – was employed by the government to produce working models for training in the use of a variety of products. These included a trench-digging tank and the sectional Inglis and later Bailey bridges, along with a railway bridge design that could be used to cross bomb craters or canals. Later in the war, they would prove instrumental in the creation of the Mulberry Harbours used after the D-Day landings, temporary, prefabricated harbours towed across the Channel to help with offloading cargo for the Allied troops fighting their way through Normandy.

Sywell airport, initially a training facility for the RAF, trained pilots to fly using Tiger Moths and later helped train the 'Free French' pilots after the fall of France. It also became the centre for the repair of Wellington bombers, the component parts needed being repaired and resupplied by a variety of Northamptonshire companies and garages scattered around the county. The parts were brought to Sywell for assembly, and the aircraft were then test flown and eventually returned to flying operations. Camouflaged hangars were also built to facilitate the assembling of Lancaster bombers, with the manufacture of parts carried out at a number of other factories, including Barratts' shoes and Northampton's tram sheds.

Wellingborough Gas Works produced gas for barrage balloons. British Timken, originally based in Birmingham, opened a new factory in Duston after heavy bombing in the Midlands necessitated a move to safeguard some key areas of its business. Northampton was deemed a safer location and less likely to be hit by the Luftwaffe. Charles Wicksteed & Co, on Digby Street, Kettering, produced hydraulic hacksaws, power tools and industrial sawing machines for the Ministry of Defence and the Royal Navy.

The Agricultural College at Moulton, Northampton.

Industries across the county were therefore vital to the continuation of the war, with thousands of men and women employed in them. At this stage of the war, a large proportion of that workforce were women. They had moved into most industries as men joined the services, and were an accepted and absolutely crucial part of the labour force, nowhere more so than in agriculture. The register that had been started in 1939 was now fully implemented, with the Women's Land Army operating all across Northamptonshire. According to published figures in 1941, their wage was 28s. (£1.40) a week. From this sum, the women had to pay for board and lodgings, sometimes on-site but in the main provided by the county at some twenty hostels (Nissan huts), each hostel generally under the control of the YMCA and managed by an older woman. Apart from controlling the day-to-day activities, this woman's responsibility also included ensuring daily time sheets were maintained and delivered to Northampton's County Hall, where a team calculated the weekly net pay. No women were allowed onto a farm until training had been completed at Moulton's Institute of Agriculture. There, as it had been in 1914–18, they were taught the rudimentary skills of farm work, particularly milking and animal husbandry. The work was hard – a forty-eight-hour week the norm – conditions generally poor and little time was allowed for the social niceties. But they proved successful, as they had in engineering, the railways, bus service, post office and various other roles, often overcoming prejudice along the way. As a workforce, they were going to be needed more and more.

But January 1941 was not just about the war. Newspapers announced the death in Nyeri, Kenya, of Lord Baden Powell, aged 84, the man responsible for the formation of the boy scouts. Also, one of the world's great aviators, Amy Johnson, was killed after crashing in the Thames Estuary. Amy, known world-wide after becoming the first woman to fly solo from Britain to Australia, was more famous locally when she landed her plane in a field beside Glendon bridge in 1931 after she had been unable to put down at Sywell due to fog. Huge crowds cheered her eventual arrival in Kettering, and again when she was guest of honour in 1932 at Northants Aero Club, where she flew in with husband Jim Mollison, another record-breaking aviator. Killed whilst flying for the Air Transport Auxiliary, her body was never recovered. She had been an inspiration to thousands and had featured in numerous cinema newsreels. Today, the circumstances of her death remain unresolved; in 1941, she was simply another casualty of war.

When Amy Johnson launched her career, flying had been in its infancy. At the time of her death, a key part of the country's defence was in the hands of the RAF. Unsurprisingly, the Battle of Britain had taken its toll on the service and there was a real need to train new pilots. In Northamptonshire, a plan was announced that would establish the first Air Training Scheme for boys aged 16–18. Wellingborough had been one of the first public schools in the country to form an air section designed to aid pupils who wished to take up careers in the RAF. The new scheme was built on the back of that organization, and was intended to teach anyone interested in a flying career the theory of flight, navigation, aircraft engine construction and operation, airmanship and the mechanics of building airframes. It proved ideal as a comprehensive pre-course for anyone looking to build a flying career, and was welcomed by the RAF as a way of stimulating interest in the service and an aid to recruitment.

In the following years, it was going to be needed. However, in early 1941 the losses suffered by the RAF during the previous summer had been addressed. Fighter Command had increased the number of pilots and aircraft, and the Luftwaffe had begun to restrict its bombing activity to night-time raids. But these attacks were still having a major impact. Key cities and industrial areas were still being targeted, and in light of Northamptonshire's growing importance – particularly in repairing bombers – raids were constantly expected. At Weldon in early February, people got their first close-up view of a German bomber when one was shot down by night fighters, killing all the crew. They were buried in Weldon shortly afterwards, their bodies eventually exhumed and returned to Germany in 1963.

In Kettering, a German Messerschmitt, complete with the bullet holes that had brought it down, had been recovered virtually in one piece and was brought into town and placed in the market square. People flocked to see it, which was the intention, as it was used as an exhibit in aid of the town's War Weapons Week. The authorities wanted to show people why the country needed to continue raising money. To this end, the Messerschmitt was a good example of Germany's aggression and firepower. In support of the appeal, in which the town had set a target of raising £250,000 (it eventually achieved £284,000), the council organized a parade of Home Guard, ARP, Fire Brigade, the town band and Salvation Army. Northampton, with its greater population, had already contributed, and throughout February the German fighter was used in several other locations, including Wellingborough, Irchester, Irthlingborough, Rushden, Higham Ferrers and Daventry, as they ran their own War Weapons Week. It was an obvious success, with well in excess of £1 million raised by the start of the spring.

This money was going to be needed. In the North African desert, after the successes at the start of the year, fortunes had changed. The Italians had been reinforced with hardened German troops and a new German commander, Lieutenant General Erwin Rommel. The British, faced with this much stronger force, were pushed back. So began the long desert war of attack and retreat, gain and loss, and desert battles synonymous with the place names around them – Tobruk, Benghazi, Sidi Barrani and El Alamein – and of course the troops who fought in them: the Desert Rats, the Afrika Korps and the Aussies (the 9th Australian Division, otherwise known as the Rats of Tobruk). Further reverses were suffered by British forces in Greece, where, after Mussolini's failed attack in 1940, British and Australian reinforcements had been sent to help the Greek army fight off any invasion by Germany. However, when the German attack came they proved ineffective, unable to mount any viable defence, and were eventually forced to evacuate. A confident Hitler then attacked Crete. Falsely thought to be well-defended by British and Commonwealth troops, it too fell quickly, to a combined attack by German paratroopers and glider-borne troops.

Good news was in short supply in 1941. Northampton's St Andrew's Hospital was badly bombed, with a large section of the infirmary completely destroyed and further damage inflicted on the other side of Billing Road in the cemetery. On 9 April, German bombs fell on Woodford, and just days later, Northampton's Billing Flax Mills were also bombed, causing significant damage, though not without some loss to the Luftwaffe. A German Heinkel bomber, caught in searchlights, was shot down over Kettering, crashing in flames near the crematorium, killing three of the crew, with the other two taken prisoner.

At sea, news had been released of the sinking of Britain's largest battlecruiser, HMS *Hood*, by the German battleship the *Bismarck*, killing 1,400 of her crew. It was an action later made famous by the 1960 British war film, *Sink the Bismarck,* starring Kenneth More. Revenge was gained forty-eight hours later after air torpedo attacks by Fairey Swordfish biplanes from the aircraft carrier HMS *Ark Royal* managed to disable the *Bismarck*'s rudder, which enabled British ships to catch and destroy her.

Despite these reverses, things were slowly beginning to improve. The war at sea to protect vital supplies reaching our shores, the Battle of the Atlantic, was beginning to turn in Britain's favour. In early May, the British destroyer HMS *Bulldog* attacked a German U-boat and forced it to the surface. The German captain's intended scuttling of his boat failed, and a boarding party seized his code books and, more importantly, the machine that deciphered the messages he received, the Enigma machine. This meant that the Admiralty was eventually able to route convoys around and away from the German submarine wolf packs. Shipping losses improved significantly, and the vital volume of imported goods reaching British shores was maintained.

President Roosevelt also signed the Lend-Lease Bill in America, which allowed Britain to obtain food, oil, warships, weaponry and other goods from the United States without payment. This was significant from Churchill's point of view because in many ways it ended America's neutrality and allowed Britain to obtain supplies at a crucial time financially for the country. Since the summer of 1940, the two countries had worked closely together. Britain in fact had supplied the USA with technical and scientific information gained through its own research and development programmes, which it had unfortunately been unable to fully exploit. This expertise allowed the Americans to fully develop its potential for their own advancement.

At a more local level, an initiative was set up in the county to begin collecting blood. Three doctors and four nurses began a round of village visits, starting at Paulerspury, then moving across most Northamptonshire villages. The aim was to create a sustainable blood bank. The Institute of Agriculture, based at Moulton, also began a programme to help Northamptonshire's farmers to better understand how to grow and manage crops of sugar beet. Local newspapers like the *Mercury & Herald* began a programme of gardening education. The plan was to educate households in the techniques used to grow home-based crops. Potatoes, for example, were considered part of a staple diet. Plans had already been put in motion to increase the amount of available land to farmers from 2,000 to 6,500 acres. What was also needed was increased input from as many homes as possible to begin a grow-your-own vegetable plot. From there it was hoped households would begin to grow a range of seasonal vegetables, much as had happened in the 1914–18 war. The newspapers tried to impart as much information as possible about how to go about setting up these plots. Vegetables were not rationed, so were ideal to grow in quantity. Elsewhere, the National Union of Boot and Shoe Operatives agreed to increase their working week from forty-five to forty-eight hours, with an agreed overtime rate to be paid for the extra three hours. Northamptonshire's Women's Voluntary Services Organization began receiving gifts of clothing from America at their distribution centre at County Hall. These were distributed across the county for the use of evacuees. According to their own reports, the quality of the clothing arriving through the American branch of the Red

Cross was first-class. So was the van provided by the Americans for use in ferrying the clothing around the county.

The Americans were proving good neighbours to have, but at this point Britain was still very much alone in a Europe at war, and mainly under the control of Hitler's armies. To try to ensure that Northamptonshire had access to vital help if and when needed, it entered into a mutual assistance pact with all its local towns and some in nearby counties. In essence, the idea was that each would provide extra labour and equipment to any that needed it for first aid and bomb damage. Those inside the county that agreed – Northampton, Wellingborough, Kettering, Rushden and Daventry – were joined by Biggleswade, Sandy, Leighton Buzzard, Hitchen, Ampthill, Dunstable, Bedford and Luton. Each appointed a liaison officer to co-ordinate any help required and ensure the system was effective. It meant there was always access to help within Northamptonshire for any serious eventuality. It was a sound idea that, as far as can be ascertained, was never called into action, though it probably got close to implementation when the silos at Whitworth Bros Flour Mills at Wellingborough caught fire on 19 June. The massive fire attracted hundreds of people onto the banks of the River Nene just to watch as it destroyed tons of stored wheat. The flames were fought for several hours by the fire services from Wellingborough, Irchester and Northampton.

The same fire services were out again a few weeks later when an RAF Stirling bomber crashed into the centre of Northampton. The four-engine aircraft, with a wingspan of 99ft (30.5m), created a massive amount of damage, particularly around Gold Street and George Row, but caused only one casualty on the ground, a man on fire-watch who was caught in the blast and suffered a broken leg. The pilot, Flight Sergeant Bernard Madgwick, was killed when his parachute failed to open, but the other six members of his crew all bailed out and survived. The plane had left Oakington on 14 July at 11 pm to carry out a bombing raid over Europe, during which it was badly damaged by flak, running out of fuel on its return over Northampton at around 5 am. At the time, of course, this information would not have been made available, but the wreckage told its own story. It was a lucky escape for the town; the Stirling still had unexploded bombs on board when it came down, one being discovered lodged in a bedroom of the Queen's

The aftermath of the Stirling bomber crash on Gold Street in 1941 (Northampton Central Library).

Head Hotel on the corner of College Street. There is little doubt it could have been a far worse tragedy than it was when the RAF arrived to remove the wreckage and its payload.

But it was not only the war that caused havoc across the county. Nature too made an impact in July 1941, with one of the biggest storms ever seen in Northamptonshire. Over a twenty-four hour period, thunderstorms wreaked havoc over a wide swath of the county, the most severe damage reserved for Northampton itself. High winds brought down half a dozen trees in Abington Park and severely damaged another ten. Others were felled on Park Avenue South, Wheatfield Road, The Avenue, Spinney Hill and Kettering Road, and a number of sheep were killed on Kingsthorpe Golf Course. Most of the town's telephone lines were brought down. The area around St Leonards Road was severely flooded, numerous houses were hit by lightning, as was the Town Hall, and roads around the north of the county became impassable. It was a timely reminder that the power of man could be more than matched by the power of the weather.

Understanding the war and its progress, as summer moved into autumn, was not easy. Cinema audiences across Northamptonshire, like elsewhere in the country, watched newsreels of Germany's advances, saw first-hand the effects of bombing raids on British cities and heard the broadcasts of Winston Churchill. At home, people listened to Lord Haw Haw on the radio. Newspapers kept people up to date with world news as best they could, informing them of the latest developments in the war. But for many, nothing they saw, read or heard told them whether the threat of invasion was still real and what would happen next? Hitler's armies had by this time opened up the Eastern Front when they attacked Russia in the summer of 1941, and had achieved considerable success as Operation Barbarossa developed. The talking points in works canteens and debates over a pint in pubs, in light of this development, were whether or not any future invasion of the British mainland was likely. What no-one realized at the time was that the invasion of Russia was really the turning point of the war.

For the British government, whilst this new war in the east took the pressure off the country, it was the Japanese attack on the US naval base at Pearl Harbor in Hawaii on 7 December that rekindled the belief in an eventual Allied victory. Willingly or not, America was about to be dragged into the European war. Germany declared war on the USA four days after Pearl Harbor, essentially ensuring their future defeat, though there were still disasters to come. The Japanese attack on the American fleet also meant Britain's Empire in the Far East was suddenly vulnerable. By the end of the second week of December, HMS *Prince of Wales* and HMS *Repulse* had been sunk off the Malayan peninsula by Japanese air attack. Singapore was also under threat and on Christmas Day Hong Kong surrendered to the victorious Japanese army. Nearer home, in the Western Desert, the war was also still far from being resolved.

There was much to do before the war would be brought to an end, and a very real need to remain alert. To that end, Northamptonshire mounted another large-scale exercise involving the Home Guard, RAF, Civil Defence and this time around 50,000 troops. The plan was to replicate the conditions that would prevail under an invasion. Roads across the county were closed off or traffic halted at various checkpoints, machine-gun posts manned, armoured vehicles moved to key points around the county, obstructions were placed on golf courses to prevent enemy planes landing, all travel was severely restricted and hospitals placed on emergency standby.

The exercise was hailed a success, and the year ended with perhaps a little more confidence in the future than had been there when it started. But with Japanese involvement the war had become more expansive, and by the close of 1941 the conflict could rightly be deemed to have become a 'world war' on an epic scale.

CHAPTER FOUR

1942
Seeing it Through

As 1942 dawned, newspaper headlines hitting the doormats of homes across the county carried the undisputable truth that Japan had seized the initiative in the Far East. Britain's Empire was being assaulted by a series of co-ordinated, well-executed attacks by the Japanese military, perhaps demonstrating just how weak that Empire actually was. Throughout January, concerted Japanese attacks successfully overran Malaya and the Philippines, forced the British to fall back in Burma and cut off Singapore. Other assaults by air and sea were reported from New Guinea and the Solomon Islands, which put Australia at risk of invasion. Japan was clearly in the ascendancy. So was Rommel out in the deserts of North Africa. Earlier British successes were nullified after the Afrika Korps retook Benghazi and began to move on Egypt. America may have entered the war and Hitler's armies been brought to a standstill in Russia, but clearly, as people digested the news every morning at the start of 1942, it was far too early to set aside all fears of an invasion on home shores.

Yet life across Northamptonshire went on as normal. Rushden held a 'Works Wonders' concert at the town's Royal Theatre, essentially a local talent show where a packed house listened to a variety of talents. The stars of the show were three sopranos representing Wellingborough, Irthlingborough and Bozeat. The Army held its inter-regimental boxing finals at the Windmill Hall, with the Hussars beating the Inniskilling Dragoons by seven events to four. George Formby's new film, *It's Turned Out Nice Again*, played the cinemas in Wellingborough and Northampton, and Tubby Turner starred in *Babes in the Wood* at Kettering. The mood, it's fair to say, remained optimistic, despite the obvious underlying tensions.

So much so that in Northampton a long debate took place in council chambers about the value of what was known as The Atlantic Charter, in essence a joint declaration made between Winston Churchill and American President Roosevelt, drawn up in August 1941. The charter outlined their vision of the world after the war, what they envisaged would make the world a safer place, allow freedom, global trade, improved economic and social conditions, and much more. These intentions had already been discussed and the main principles agreed by all the governments in exile as far back as September. The final document, signed on 1 January 1942 by all in agreement under the title of Declaration by United Nations, would eventually form the basis for what we know today as the UN. In Northampton, a debate led by two MPs with opposing views debated its content, under the watchful eye of the town's Lord Mayor, Alderman Bugby. Reported by the *Northamptonshire Evening Telegraph*, it gave people an opportunity to understand, perhaps in greater detail, the charter that had been much written about since its inception by the two leaders of the free world.

Elsewhere, the debate was about the shortage of paper and the need to recycle if the newspaper industry was to continue unaffected by the war. Collections had already been organized across the county by soldiers stationed locally, and by mid-January 1942 some 5 tons had been secured from households and businesses. However, there was a genuine need to significantly increase this amount. To that end, various articles had been written and circulars distributed to inform people of the very real shortages caused by a lack of resources. The response was positive, but paper at that time was often put to use in the home. Most houses across the county were heated by coal or coke fires; old newspapers helped light the morning fire, so recycling was always going to be problematical. In many ways a lesser problem was the national scrap metal campaign, which had been in operation for some time and, according to the county council, had proven extremely successful. Even St Giles' church, Northampton, had given up its railings, though we know today that much of the metal collection was never reused and was largely a government ploy to boost morale at a time when it was felt people needed to feel they were all contributing to the war effort.

In the east of the county, the headlines were grabbed by the announcement that Higham Ferrers had been gifted a £10,000 Town Hall and chains of office for the Mayoress and Deputy Mayoress by Mr John White, a local employer, the owner of John White Footwear Ltd and much respected in the town and surrounding area. He had already contributed £5,000, raised by himself and his workforce, to buy a Spitfire, which was given the name 'Impregnable', and he was keen for the council to have access to improved facilities despite the war. It was a munificent gift from a man who would go on to benefit the area in a variety of ways over the following years.

More good news came with the public announcement that a member of the Wellingborough Home Guard was to receive an award for gallantry. In June the previous year, an empty wagon train had pulled into the sidings at Wellingborough, having travelled from London during the night whilst the capital was being bombed. Company Sergeant Major Orton, working in the sidings at the time, noticed that one of the empty wagons had been hit by two bombs, neither of which had exploded and remained in situ. Realizing the danger they posed, he ran across to where the train had stopped, removed both unexploded bombs and carried them to a place of safety. The unassuming sergeant, who had served in the Northants Regiment during the 1914–18 war, said when interviewed, 'It was nothing.' But it led, deservedly, to him being the first in the county to receive an award for gallantry.

This incident was a timely reminder that despite the war raging out in the Far East and across Russia, there was still real danger here at home. The Luftwaffe had not given up on their bombing attacks on Britain, and air raids were still seen as a very real and potent threat. With that in mind, the county council announced at the beginning of February that a new type of air raid shelter would be made available. Named after the Minister of Home Security, Herbert Morrison, this was an indoor shelter designed as a secure cage with a steel table top. Measuring 6ft 6in (2m) by 4ft (1.2m) wide x 2ft 6in (0.75m) high, it was intended to be used inside a house to withstand a bomb blast that brought down the upper floors. Essentially, it was designed for use by those who had been unable to erect an Anderson shelter and lived in a house without a cellar. The cage allowed people to sleep inside it during the night and remain safe if bombing brought down part of the house in which they lived. It was free to all those dependant on earnings of not more than £350 a year (plus £50 per annum per child), or could be purchased for around £7. The self-assembly structures were seen as effective, though were probably not widely used across Northamptonshire.

By this stage of the war, air raids across the county had been few and far between, with most of the bombing centred around the major cities. The notion that everyone needed an air raid shelter or home protection was probably not seen as crucial, at least not as it had been in the early years of the war. What was viewed with a greater sense of urgency, certainly by the government, was the need to bring more women into war work. Loudspeaker vans had toured the county since the start of the year, audiences at cinemas were openly addressed before the start of the film show and Women's War Job Bureaux had been set up in Northampton, Kettering and Wellingborough. The intention was to educate women in the need for more munitions and how they could help. Enlisting local newspapers, the various councils across Northamptonshire began to run articles about the advantages, both to the country and to the women who agreed to sign up. The stumbling block for many was that they had to move away from home. For many women it meant living in a hostel (purpose-built Nissan huts in some cases), though sometimes the women stayed in private houses costing around 25s. a week, with room-sharing common practice and long working hours the norm, which in turn made for a long working week. Most women working in munitions, according to the *Northamptonshire Evening Telegraph*, had only a long weekend (Saturday and Sunday) off every third week, along with one week's holiday a year, and the pay was not especially high. The *Northamptonshire Evening Telegraph*, perhaps a little suspicious of claims being made on pay and in order to avoid any misunderstanding, published the government's pay rates for women:

Royal Ordnance (munitions)

16–18 years old	shift mornings only	£1 14s. 4d.
18 years old	shift 2.45–10.15 pm	£2 13s. 5d.
	shift 8.45 am–7.15 pm	£3 6s. 4d.

19 years old	shift 6.45 am–3.15 pm	£2 19s. 11d.
	shift 2.45 pm–10.15 pm	£2 15s. 11d.
	shift 8.45 am–7.15 pm	£3 9s. 6d.
	shift 6.45 am–3.15 pm	£2 18s. 5d.
20 years old	shift 2.45 pm–10.15 pm	£2 18s. 5d.
	shift 8.45 am–7.15 pm	£3 12s. 8d.
	shift 6.45 am–3.15 pm	£2 14s. 7d.
21 years old +	shift 2.45 pm–10.15 pm	£3 1s. 0d.
	shift 8.45 am–7.15 pm	£3 15s. 10d.
	shift 6.45 am–3.15 pm	£2 16s. 11d.

For those who decided against this kind of work, there was always conscription. The National Service Act had been passed in December 1941, making the conscription of women legal. In February 1942, childless and single women aged between 20–30 (changed to 19–43 later in the war) were told to report to their local office of the Ministry of Labour. There, they were given the option of entering one of the armed forces or going into industry or farming. Many decided to join the various service ranks. Others went into occupations such as aircraft production, engineering, the Land Army or the police. The Women's Auxiliary Police Corps was formed to help supplement the police service, which had been struggling to maintain full strength. Across the county, due to men leaving to enlist in the services, the police had been drawing manpower from three areas: the police reserve, recently retired police officers who had contracted to return to the force in the event of war; Special constabulary, a peacetime voluntary additional force of trained, uniformed officers; and finally the Police War Reserve. The latter was set up in 1939 and consisted of men over the age of 30 who had agreed to serve in the force for the duration of the war. These initiatives, whilst helping maintain numbers, were not sufficient to keep pace with the administration required by a police service operating in wartime conditions. The decision to bring in women was taken because of the need to take over these clerical, administrative duties, not to allow them to become fully trained police officers – that would take a few more years.

The way the war was progressing, despite American involvement, it looked as if it would continue for several more years. Headlines in newspapers and broadcasts on the radio brought little good news. Japan was still in the ascendency. Singapore fell on 14 February and the Japanese navy defeated an Allied naval force in the Battle of the Java Sea. A combined naval and RAF attempt to sink the German battleships *Scharnhorst* and *Gneisenau* as they made a dash through the Channel failed. It was clearly going to take more than bravery and resolve to defeat the forces of Hitler and Emperor Hirohito. Losses

Warship Week, as advertised in Burton Latimer.

had to be made good, lost weapons replaced and warships rebuilt. The government needed money. Since the start of the war, fundraising efforts across the county had been substantial. People had raised funds to buy Spitfires, increased those funds to buy new weapons, and now they embarked upon Warships Week. The idea, supported across the shire, was to raise finance for the Navy, with towns and villages attempting to raise enough money through the purchasing of government savings certificates to either buy or adopt a warship.

Wellingborough, Irthlingborough and surrounding villages aimed at raising £280,000. Thrapston, where a mock-up of a prow of a battleship was set up in the market place, attempted to raise £72,000 and adopt a motor torpedo boat. Isham targeted

£2,000. Kettering, in conjunction with Burton Latimer, Corby, Desborough, Rothwell and some thirty smaller villages, aimed to raise £250,000. Oundle aimed for £120,000, Northampton and the surrounding villages set out to raise in excess of £300,000, while Rushden, Higham Ferrers and Raunds combined efforts to pull in over £250,000. So it went on across the county, and all successfully exceeded their targets. This was done through a combination of funds raised by street savings clubs, house-to-house canvassing, parades in towns, fetes, dances, businesses creating their own savings groups and individuals buying through post offices and banks and by involving organizations like the ATC, Women's Land Army, Fire Brigade and the WVS. The county worked very much as a team, all determined to succeed, and it worked.

But it was not just money that was needed. Farmers were looking at ways to improve and increase crop yields, not just in cereal crops but also in grassland management for dairy herds. At Oundle, one of the first educational and instructional meetings was held in the Victoria Hall. Set up by the government under the auspices of the NFU (National Farmers' Union) and the Ministry of Agriculture, its intention was to help farmers improve the way they cultivated their land. Since the start of the war, the country had never succeeded in creating large reserves of imported feedstuffs such as barley, maize and oilseeds. What the Ministry wanted to do was increase crop yields in these areas in order that dairy herds produced more milk. With meat becoming ever more scarce, milk was seen as vital. To that end, they were trying to impress upon the farming community that each farm must be able to provide its own feedstuffs. Reliance upon imports, in light of the German U-boat campaign, no longer guaranteed continuity of supply. What was proposed was ley farming, an old system of agriculture used by farms with large areas of grassland. It was essentially a method of using land initially for cash crops, then allowing it to lie fallow to grow hay, seed crops or as pasture for a number of years. According to the Northants War Agricultural Committee, this system and seed crop variations would enable farms to become self-sufficient and increase the milk yield in most locations across the county. As other meetings followed across the shire, this approach became the predominant message, and new, different crops began to appear as the year went on, one of which was sunflowers.

Instructional, informative meetings were not only taking place for farming. There was a recognition by the government and a locally identified need by Northamptonshire County Council that a new arm of the civil defence needed to be formed. Firebomb raids by the Luftwaffe had become ever more prevalent in some parts of the country. As a result, widespread fires often caused more damage than high explosive blasts. It was therefore decided to form a Fire Guard (similar to the Fire-Watchers). These would be volunteers, working closely with the ARP, who would be trained to deal with and extinguish firebombs as they fell. Sand had already been distributed all around the county, as had stirrup pumps in many locations, but there had been no concerted effort to organize small, dedicated teams to handle this type of incendiary bombing. Titchmarsh, on the eastern edge of the county, had already been firebombed, as had Lowick, where around 300 incendiaries fell, and various other villages across the county, so there was clearly a need. Time was the key element, something volunteers had to give up, often after a long working day, and often not so easily spared, particularly when the work frequently entailed a great deal of tedious waiting and watching. Nevertheless, people did come forward, many of them women, and watches were set at various locations in villages and towns across the county.

There was still a feeling they would be needed, as news of the war showed no signs of improvement. Allied troops were forced to surrender in Borneo. Though it was quieter over London, German bombers had devastated the cities of Exeter, Bath, Norwich, York and Canterbury, and shipping losses caused by attacks from the German submarine fleet still severely affected food supplies. By the spring, the only measurable success seemed to be courtesy of the RAF. Air Marshal Arthur 'Bomber' Harris was appointed Commander in Chief of Bomber Command at the end of February. At the end of May, he launched a 1000 bomber raid against the German city of Cologne. Widely reported at the time, the bombers had spent seventy-five minutes over the city, completely destroying its centre. Of course it was a one-off, because Bomber Command could not sustain raids on this scale; that would come later. Nevertheless, it lifted morale at home, as it had been intended to do, and showed how vulnerable Germany could be. As did the news that, two months earlier, British commandos, along with volunteers from the Royal Navy, had successfully attacked the dry dock at Saint-Nazaire in north-western France, using a ship packed with explosives, which exploded twenty-four hours later and put the dock out of action for the remainder of the war.

As a result, the mood across Northamptonshire, as thousands lined the streets of the county's town in celebration of United Nations Day, was perhaps more optimistic than it had been earlier in the year. Certainly, the extent of the celebrations and the general enthusiasm were good indicators that this was the case. Marchers and bands paraded through Northampton, Rushden, Wellingborough, Daventry and Kettering. Thousands gathered to listen to speeches from a variety of dignitaries and representatives of various religious denominations. The Home Guard turned out across the shire, as did the Fire Service, the nurses, the ARP, police and various arms of the Civil Defence. Flags adorned public buildings, the Prime Minister's message of hope was read to the crowds and everyone ended the day with a rendition of the national anthem. But there were still dark days ahead.

Japan had attacked the American fleet out in the Coral Sea, and Burma had finally fallen as the British fell back into India. Rommel had swept across the Libyan desert into Egypt, pushing the British and their Allies back, and on 21 June Tobruk had been taken by the Afrika Korps. Only the advance of the Russian army on the Eastern Front offered up the promise of a German defeat, and that seemed to have stalled. So, despite the good weather, there was still much to do. But the Americans were coming.

At the start of July, the 97th Bombardment Group of the United States Army Air Force (USAAF) took over the RAF airfield at Polebrook, east Northamptonshire. Originally built by George Wimpey as a training base, it had been in operational use by the RAF's 90 Squadron until it was decided it would better suit the needs of the Americans. They also took over the RAF bomber airfield at Grafton Underwood, which was essentially a satellite of Polebrook and had three runways which could handle the American B-17Es. Their first bombing run was made in August when they attacked the marshalling yards at Rouen.

Protection in the form of decoy airfields had already been set up at Warmington in 1941. The idea behind this was to create the impression, at least from the air, that Warmington had an

A pillbox as it looks today at Polebrook airfield.

operational airfield which would be hit by the Luftwaffe rather than the real airfields at Polebrook and Grafton. It was a clever idea that involved ground personnel setting up lights that would mimic aircraft landing lights. These were then moved around to simulate aircraft on the ground. The tactic was initially successful but, as the war went on and the German pilots became more skilful, its usefulness diminished and it was eventually abandoned.

All this enterprise and the running of the war was costing money. Exactly how much was published by the *Northamptonshire Evening Telegraph* when it reported on the speech made by the Chancellor of the Exchequer, Sir Kingsley Wood, who addressed Parliament in the middle of the summer. According to his figures, the war was costing the country £84,250,000 every week, and since it had begun in 1939 had cost the staggering sum of £8,600,000,000. In his words: 'This is by far the costliest war in history … but this does not dismay us. There will be no faltering in the financial or any other sphere, and the task of financing the war will not dismay us.' It put into perspective the need for all the fundraising efforts

Wellingborough after the first August 1942 air raid (Northampton Central Library).

that had gone on throughout the first half of the year, and would continue throughout the war.

If there were any people with doubts that this was a just war, then Bank Holiday Monday, 3 August, dispelled them. At 6.10 pm the sirens went off in Wellingborough. Within minutes of the alarm being sounded, a German bomber, flying low over the town, dropped four high-explosive bombs. They fell over the shops, houses and businesses opposite the Hind Hotel, in Midland Road, Newcombe Road and Winstanley Road. Four women, two men and one boy were killed, twenty-three women, twenty-one men, five boys and six girls being injured. The destruction was extensive, with some forty-three homes seriously damaged and 388 badly damaged, along with ten factories, half a dozen churches, thirteen hotels and pubs, 125 shops, two cinemas and five banks. Fortunately, most people were on the outskirts of town at the bank holiday fair, as otherwise casualties could have been far greater. It took until 10 August to clear the debris, but twelve days later the Luftwaffe were back.

On 22 August at 10.53 pm precisely, the alert sounded again. Almost at the same time, bombs fell in Swanspool Gardens, Dulley's Yard, in Sheep Street, Midland Road and the junction of Alma Road and Park Road. A member of the Home Guard was killed and twenty-five

More extensive damage to Wellingborough after August 1942's air raids (Northampton Central Library).

people injured. One hundred and four houses were damaged, along with a cafe, forty-five shops, two cinemas, five factories, the GPO, the Council Offices and the HQ of the 7th Northamptonshire Battalion of the Home Guard in Dulley's Yard, which was being used to store ammunition and phosphorus bombs. This time casualties were lower and damage less severe, the impact perhaps being more on morale. The summer on the home front across Northamptonshire had been quiet, but the raids were a reminder that there was still a long way to go before the war was won and the danger of attacks from the air became a thing of the past. But Churchill's visit to the desert that same August and the promotion of Lieutenant General Bernard Montgomery to the command of the Eighth Army would go some way toward shortening that journey.

Montgomery was not then particularly well known back in Britain, and history records that Churchill had his doubts about the appointment to succeed Claude Auchinleck. But he was a meticulous commander of men and exhibited a determination to win the desert war that impressed those around him. For the Prime Minister, the instructions to his new commander were probably relatively brief. Britain needed a victory, and the expectation was that he would deliver it. Back at home, where the newspaper headlines over the past year had seemingly reported on nothing but defeat and retreat in the Middle East, most would have agreed with the same sentiment. There had been little to cheer about over the last few months, and a little good news would go a long way. It would come, but not for a while yet.

The pressing issues for Northamptonshire during the summer were mainly centred around education and evacuees. The matters went hand-in-hand. After the influx of evacuees back in 1939, there had been a comprehensive plan to deal with the numbers arriving. At the end of that year and through the early part of 1940, many of these same evacuees, mainly from the London area, had returned home. Pressure on schools and housing therefore eased. But the Blitz and more concentrated German bombing in the south re-inflated the numbers of evacuees, and schools in particular were finding it difficult to cope. According to the Northants Education Committee, at the start of spring 1942 there were around 8,100 evacuees in Northamptonshire occupying school places. With them also came an increase in childhood ailments and general issues of uncleanliness. So much so, that the Ministry of Health and London County Council decided that no child could be evacuated from the London area suffering from scabies or other skin diseases within the previous four weeks, or found with vermin, nits, abrasions, lesions or scratches.

Not that many travelling children were found to be infected in this way, but those who were had obviously increased the risk to local children, which in turn spread any infection with greater rapidity than would have otherwise happened. But, according to the Education Committee's report, a far greater problem existed in providing adequate meals at the schools the evacuees attended. This necessity caused an increase in expenditure, as would have been expected, but to a far greater level than had been planned. In essence, schools across the county had insufficient room to set up proper catering facilities. This meant that they were using outside resources. At Paulerspury, for example, the local school commandeered the Parish rooms. Walgrave, Gretton and Broughton were forced to open canteens nearby. Corby, Daventry and Rushden schools that could accommodate the numbers had problems of a different nature, based around cost. And so it went on across the whole county, each area with its own set of problems, many of which would not be easily resolved. But as a result of the Education Committee's assessment of the situation, more money was made available for the rest of the year and central cooking depots were set up, which took the pressure off the smaller schools and were more able to produce and deliver meals within reasonable budgets that were more easily managed.

The bonus of having a significant number of children in the county was that those of secondary school age, who were able, could be utilized as labour on local farms, something many schoolchildren had done since the start of the war; they provided, at times, a much-needed boost to the available manpower. In 1939 there was some 112,300 acres of arable land in Northamptonshire; by 1942, the acreage had increased by a staggering 115 per cent. The knock-on effect of this was that farmers could increase the yield of some key crops. Potatoes were grown in far larger quantities than at any time previously, simply because more acreage was available. Sugar beet harvests grew along similar lines. The children's help proved crucial, as was that of the Women's Land Army, which was able to supply around 1,000 women to Northamptonshire farms. Any extra help, particularly at harvest time, was supplied by the

Army, though as the war moved into a more offensive phase this help would become limited.

So it was not all bad news. Also helping to lift morale locally was The Duchess of Gloucester, who paid a visit to the industrial areas around Wellingborough and the Maison de Convalescence, Broad Green (known locally as Spring Hill), just outside the town. The convalescence home, run by Madame Jeanne Mitchell, a French military nurse who had been awarded the Croix de Guerre, housed thirty-six patients. Originally set up by Madame Mitchell and her husband to house evacuees, she had converted it to help French soldiers wounded in the war after Dunkirk and the fall of France. According to reports, the Duchess had a perfect command of French and was able to talk to the patients in their native language as she moved around the hospital before stepping out to meet the hundreds who lined the streets as news of her arrival spread around the town. For many, the visit was a welcome distraction in the middle of what was proving to be a long war.

In late October came the news that everyone had been watching and waiting for. The new commander of the Eighth Army finally made his move. The Battle of El Alamein had begun. Kept up to date by national and local newspapers, along with radio broadcasts, homes across the county followed the action as best they could, all too well aware this was a battle on a massive scale and the future of the war, certainly in North Africa, depended upon its outcome. It was more than ten days before they knew its result and could openly celebrate an Allied victory. Rommel was beaten, his army in full retreat and the desert war had entered its final stages. It was not known at the time just how momentous this action had been. Thousands of men, tanks and heavy guns were involved in one of the greatest land battles of the British Army, and as a consequence losses were heavy. On the home front, something had changed; optimism was back. After years of defeat and loss, the war had turned in the Allies' favour. German conquests were now at an end, and it became a matter for them of defending the Fatherland.

Remembrance Day all across the county became more meaningful as a consequence of the victory at El Alamein. Churches around Northamptonshire were full. Parades took place in the towns and people gathered around the various cenotaphs to lay wreaths. In Corby, where the numbers attending were too great for the church to hold, services were held in cinemas. The Home Guard turned out, many of them ex-servicemen, joined by the British Legion and, in places, other veterans who had fought in the Boer War at the turn of the century. For many it was not just a reminder of those who died in previous conflicts, but of those yet to be named, those on war fronts all across the world and those who paid the price of victory in the desert. As recorded by the *Northamptonshire Evening Telegraph*, it was a very poignant and moving moment in time.

But life quickly returned to normal. Iron-ore miners employed by Wellingborough Iron Co and some 460 miners working for Richard Thomas & Co of Irthlingborough went on strike two days later. Demands for increases in pay had not been met. The industrial action was short-lived – the men returned to work after twenty-four hours – but effective, an agreement being reached a week later. Elsewhere, arguments broke out between retailers selling fish. Already in short supply due to the war, the press reported on an unfair system that allowed more fish to be distributed to outlets in Wellingborough than in Kettering. This was denied by the Ministry of Food and not believed by the businesses, but it was an argument that rumbled on throughout November and December. Perhaps more keenly felt was the shortage in sweets and chocolate. Since July, only 2oz. had been allowed per person due to the shortages of sugar and manufacturers having to produce sweets using only 54 per cent of the usual amount. That had in turn also pushed up the price significantly, which meant people were not buying sweets. But Northamptonshire, or at least parts of it, had one advantage others did not at the end of 1942: the Americans began arriving, and they wanted to help out where they could.

In Kettering, American servicemen organized a Christmas party for local children, giving up one month's ration and some pay in order that they could bring sweets, cakes and chocolate to the party. They also organized a visit from Santa and gave every child attending a 1s. (5p) piece and a bag of sweets. It was a huge success and no doubt much appreciated.

As the year ended, further good news began to filter through that the Japanese advance had been stopped by a combined force of Australian and American troops that prevented the total loss of New Guinea. As local churches filled on Christmas Eve, there was a sense of optimism that at last the war had begun to turn.

CHAPTER FIVE

1943
Turning the Corner

The previous twelve months had been a roller coaster ride in many respects. At the beginning of 1942, the country was still very much on the back foot, despite the welcome news that America had joined the fight. The Axis powers (Germany, Italy and Japan) had been dominating, America in turmoil and Britain still very much isolated. At the year's end, all that had changed. The Japanese advances had stalled and the 'unbeatable' German army was in retreat on two fronts, the desert and in Russia. The time for a little positive optimism had finally arrived. However, it was not the war that grabbed the local newspaper headlines at the start of the New Year but the mysterious, sordid deaths of Rushden's most eligible and rich bachelor, Arthur Sumpter, and his housekeeper Betty Gallay (real name Betty Barratt).

Closely followed by the local press, the story gripped the public and read like a Hollywood film script. Sumpter, believed to have inherited around £30,000 in 1930, and the woman he had shared his house with, had essentially lived together in secret. Their bodies were discovered on New-Year's-Eve side by side, in an upstairs bedroom at the Rushden house he owned, The Gables. Both had been shot, she four times, he twice. A married man, Arthur Sumpter had separated from his wife and begun an affair with the live-in housekeeper. She in turn, having tired of the affair, had apparently embarked on a new relationship with a soldier stationed nearby. As the story unravelled in the press and at the inquest court, jealousy appeared to have led to the double killing. Sumpter murdered Betty in the early hours of 31 December and then supposedly shot himself shortly afterwards. The strange circumstance that surrounded the killings, and fascinated readers, was the fact that he was shot first in the shoulder, then in the head, and the revolver that fired the shots was found near his right leg, but out of reach of his hand. The Coroner brought in a verdict of suicide. The mystery was whether or not that was really true. Whatever the truth, it was the major local talking point and distraction at the start of 1943.

Yet the war was never far away. The USAAF 56th Fighter Group moved into the RAF base at Kings Cliffe, East Northants, which was initially a training base for the Americans to learn about RAF fighter-control procedures and carry out combat training. The grass runways, which had been used by the RAF when operational for Spitfires, were gradually replaced with hard surfaces. On the world stage, Churchill flew to Casablanca, where he met with President Roosevelt. Their conference was intended to decide the future conduct of the war and the strategy of the Allied forces to enable it to come out on top. Key decisions, though not announced at the time, were the invasion of Sicily, the defeat of Germany's U-boat fleet and the complete victory in the North African desert. The latter was achieved in part when Montgomery's Eighth Army succeeded in capturing Tripoli.

Here in Northamptonshire, after the Education Committee's long debate of the previous summer about childhood diseases, outbreaks of scabies were reported in larger numbers than had previously been expected, all around the county. Reports received by the county's medical officers suggested cases were on the increase, and not just amongst children newly evacuated from the south. Seen as an infestation rather than a disease, a number of cleansing stations were set up around the county and schools closely monitored. According to their report, almost all the cases recorded were in the rural areas of the county, with the worst outbreak occurring in the village of Broughton. Vigilance was the order of the day.

Elsewhere, the concerns tended to be centred on the military. The ATS (Women's Auxiliary Territorial Service) paraded in Northampton's market square. Originally a volunteer force of women who trained to take on various roles in industry, by this stage of the war the initial concept – of either becoming a cook, clerk, orderly or driver – had changed. Women began to move into more specialized and technical areas, though not all by any means. Nevertheless, their role in the war effort was increasingly vital, and they operated all across the county. Essentially an arm of the Territorial Army, they undertook six weeks' training on joining and then worked at a variety of locations. Some were based at Castle Ashby, sleeping in the house's Long Gallery, others around St Giles, Northampton, and some in Brackley, Kettering, Oundle and various places in between. In Rushden, 1,200 men made up of the Home Guard and an American contingent marched along the High Street to a church service held at the Ritz Cinema, led by the band of the 1st Northamptonshire Regiment and cheered on by huge crowds, with the Stars and Stripes flying over the town for the first time. Similar marches took place in Towcester and Daventry, where the Long Buckby Home Guard paraded its own band. In Oundle, the Home Guard, including sections from Islip, Thrapston and Aldwincle, marched alongside the RAF. All of this, of course, was intended to lift morale.

Some industries, though, needed it more than others. At the annual meeting of the Northampton Boot Manufacturers' Association, the news was less than encouraging. Productivity had fallen since the start of the war, with retail on the high street being the hardest hit. Across the whole industry in Northamptonshire, according to their report, 1942 was the hardest year for production in all factories, brought about in the main by the impact of the war across Europe and the continuing U-boat campaign mounted by the Germans against merchant shipping. Imported raw material supplies were severely affected, which in turn obviously impacted detrimentally on the home market. Productivity of boots and shoes for the high street was much curtailed so that the supply of boots to the armed forces could be maintained without interruption. Employee losses imposed on the industry by key production personnel seconded into the services or to various government projects had also not helped. Neither had a disrupted supply chain at home, caused by German bombing raids in some parts of Britain. But despite all this, the industry survived, mainly due to its solid foundations, experience learned from the First World War and by being innovative. Recycled leather was used where possible, and ladies' wood-soled footwear had been brought in to try to supplement high street fashion wear. So whilst the current state of affairs in the county was of a struggling industry, the outlook, as association president Mr Tebbutt told the assembled business owners, was extremely positive. The war, he told them, had begun to turn; the clouds were clearing and the sun was shining.

In other words, the outlook was not so bleak as it had been. Mr Tebbutt had good reason for the optimism. One thing the industry had managed to do since 1939 was to learn to work together instead of in opposition. Businesses across the county were by now working with each other and managing the problems caused by the war collectively. It was a very real positive for all concerned.

News from the war supported Mr Tebbutt's view. The German Sixth Army fighting around Stalingrad had surrendered in early February. The Russians, attacking across a wide front, had forced the Germans into retreat and eventual collapse. Out in the desert, Montgomery's Eighth Army had succeeded in pushing Rommel further back, then paused to regroup at what was known as the Mareth Line along the Tunisian and Libyan border. In the Far East, the British had formed a fighting group, the Chindits, and attacked the Japanese in Burma. So on the ground there were good reasons to be a little more optimistic. Even at sea the news filtering back was more positive than at any time during the war so far. The key enemy there of course was still the German U-boat fleet, which had proved difficult to defeat and had caused shortages in both food and materials. It was a situation that had been closely examined by that Casablanca conference. The Royal Navy began to examine an idea that would improve its fighting capability. They needed it. Germany had successfully launched around fourteen new U-boats a month into the battle to secure the Atlantic throughout the first few months of the year. If given the freedom to roam, it was pretty obvious what was likely to happen and the consequential impact on Britain's imports. Success for the Royal Navy was mainly in the deployment of submarine-hunting aircraft. But, being shore based aircraft, they had limitations based on their flying range. In order to overcome the problem, it was decided to convert a number of merchant vessels into aircraft carriers. This allowed convoys to be escorted, not only by Royal Naval destroyers and cruisers, but also by these merchant ships carrying three or four submarine-hunting aircraft. The aircraft were flown on ahead and around the convoy to find the submarines and destroy them before they could attack. It was a tactic that worked, and shipping losses reduced as a result. It was also, in part, not widely publicised at home at the time.

What was well publicized, both locally and nationally, was the air war. Bomber Command under Arthur Harris had decided to mount a concerted attempt by the Allied air forces to destroy much of Hitler's industrial and economic capability. It was hoped this would also begin to erode morale amongst the German people and weaken their fighting resolve. From the start of the year there began a series of bombing raids – the RAF bombing by night, the USAAF by day – to attack Hitler's industrial capability and a number of key towns and cities. This continued throughout 1943, with significant raids made not only on the Ruhr, which culminated in the famous Dambusters raid on 16 May, but also Hamburg, Stuttgart, Aachen, Nuremberg and Berlin. The skies above Northamptonshire were constantly full of heavy bombers, American bomber squadrons being based at Deenethorpe, Polebrook, Grafton Underwood and Chelveston, and their losses were keenly felt by the local villages.

Northamptonshire was a significant county for both the USAAF and the RAF because of its level landscape and rural position in the south of England, near to the Continent. There were seventeen airfields scattered across the county, from Peterborough in the north – which in 1943 was still a part of the shire – to Chipping Norton, Silverstone, Brackley and Croughton (which had a grass runway) in the south. RAF and American military personnel thus featured widely in many people's lives, whether on a social level or through business and trade. The pilots and crews who flew the planes, the mechanics who repaired the damage and the men and women who ran the airfields were known, many by name, and losses among them, particularly those who did the flying, were significant.

But those losses were accepted, because most people could clearly see the war was slowly beginning to turn. Across the county, people listened to the radio, read the newspapers and watched the newsreels at local cinemas. For the first time since 1939, it was becoming clear that the war, certainly across Europe, was slowly being won and that at some point in the not too distant future, Europe would be freed by the Allies. But that was still some way off. In the interim, food production was still key. The Battle for the Atlantic may have been succeeding, but there was still no significant increase in imports at this stage of the war. What proved hugely successful across Northamptonshire was farming. Since that farmers' meeting in Oundle the previous year, farms across the county had readily embraced new ideas and new technology. Since 1942, the Women's Land Army had continued to grow and this, by now, huge increase in available labour had allowed farmers to implement the concept of turning grassland into arable land.

According to a published report by the *Northampton Evening Telegraph*, farmers had finally achieved the goal of growing their own animal feeding stuffs and vastly increased the yields in arable crops such as wheat, barley, oats, potatoes and sugar beet. In turn, that increased milk production in their dairy herds, while the buying in of beef cattle from counties in the west increased meat supplies to local butchers. Land at Holdenby, Lamport, Spratton, Deene, Clopton and around the Nene was turned from grass to arable crops. The War Agricultural Committee also authorized grants to various Northampton farms to assist in the clearance of ditches and the setting up of field drainage systems. Help along the way was provided by the massive success of the government's earlier Dig For Victory campaign, which increased the number of allotments, the formation of local clubs for any wishing to rear pigs, poultry and rabbits and the launch of farm camps around the county to supply additional farm labour, with school children giving up time in their summer holidays to help in essential harvesting and other work. In the east of the county there were such camps at Achurch, Lyveden, Lilford, Apethorpe and Tansor.

While on the food side things were going reasonably well, for everything else there was always the 'black market'. It seems most people knew someone or had met someone who could find them goods that were scarce, at a price of course. How they sourced these scarce items was never enquired into, and nothing the government tried to do eradicated the market. It was simply a part of being at war. Once the Americans moved onto some of the air bases, supplies of certain goods increased. Being well provisioned by their home bases helped, as did their generosity, which meant goods in short supply to the public could, more often than not, be sourced from the USAAF. It seems few complaints were made.

As summer arrived, so another key fundraising activity began – Wings for Victory Week. Throughout June, all the towns and villages began what by this time was a familiar process, organizing parades, street collections, dances, exhibitions, garden fetes and so on in an attempt to raise significant amounts of money through the purchase of War Bonds. News of these efforts was overshadowed by the loss of the much-loved British film actor and director, Leslie Howard. A huge film star of the 1930s, Howard had featured in blockbuster films *Gone with the Wind*, *The Scarlet Pimpernel*, *The First of the Few* and *The Petrified Forest*, the latter opposite Bette Davis. He was tragically killed over the Bay of Biscay when his BOAC flight was attacked by German fighters and shot down, with the loss of all on board. Strangely coincidental was the announcement of the death of Major Martin, a man no-one knew because he never existed. Major Martin was the pseudonym given to the body of a man (Glyndwr Michael, who died in London) released off the coast of Spain. Dressed in the uniform of a major of the Royal Marines, the body, carrying maps and plans detailing a British invasion of Greece, was a brilliant piece of subterfuge intended to fool the German high command into believing Greece, not Sicily, was about to be attacked. Operation Mincemeat, as it was known in military circles, proved a huge success and caused the Germans to divert troops to the wrong place. That helped allow the invasion of Sicily to go ahead with minimal casualties. Only after the war did the significance of Major Martin's obituary become common knowledge, when the film *The Man Who Never Was* became a huge cinema success in 1956. It seems very fitting that among the cinema hits in Northamptonshire in June 1943 were *Queen of Spies* and *The Great Impersonator*.

Throughout the spring and early summer, more good news hit the headlines from the war front. Montgomery's 'Desert Rats' broke through the Mareth Line, forcing the Afrika Korps to retreat toward Tunis, where they eventually surrendered and brought the desert war to an end. Out in the East, Japan's naval commander, Admiral Yamamoto, was killed when the plane taking him to the Solomon Islands was shot down by American fighter planes. German armoured forces were defeated in Russia in the biggest tank battle in history at Prokhorovka – the culmination of Operation Citadel, the German attempt to crush the Kursk salient – and the invasion of Sicily was begun by British, Canadian and American troops, which opened the door to a further invasion on the Italian mainland. By the end of July, with the war clearly turning in the Allies' favour, Mussolini had been overthrown and imprisoned.

There was, of course, a price to pay for success, and generally that price was lives. Many soldiers had already died as a result of the war, more had been severely wounded and many thousands taken prisoner. With that in mind, the Duke and Duchess of Gloucester launched an appeal for the Red Cross at a fete held at their Northamptonshire home, Barnwell Manor. Thousands turned out to listen to a speech by Field Marshal Sir Philip Chetwode, who explained the difficulties faced by the Red Cross in a world at war. He said that over the past few years, a great deal of material had been lost due to conflict, particularly in France, Crete and Greece, and that material needed to be replaced if the organization was to continue to function effectively.

By this stage of the war, in fact, the Red Cross had raised around £20 million, but the costs of running convalescent homes for the wounded and ensuring those held in captivity had access to drugs and food parcels far exceeded this amount. As he explained to his audience, the number of prisoners captured by the Japanese was difficult to access. Earlier in the year, some 4,000 tons of much-needed medical supplies had been sent out to the Far East on ships used for the exchange of diplomats, which ensured their safe arrival. What was needed was help by the Japanese to ensure the supplies actually arrived where they were intended and needed, something he, and the Red Cross, could not guarantee. Across Europe, he added, the situation was much better. Germany accepted and transported Red Cross parcels into prisoner-of-war camps, but not so the Italians, whose organization was apparently very poor. There was so much work to do and much more money required to maintain supplies, something not lost on the crowds that enjoyed their day and gave generously, despite their own problems.

For some, however, the Red Cross was never going to be of help. In August, the *Northamptonshire Evening Telegraph* published a harrowing report of the German occupation of Russia by Alexei Tolstoy. As far as can be ascertained, this article was the first account seen in Northamptonshire of the genocide committed against the Jews and the Russian people by Hitler's forces. It told of the wanton destruction of the towns and villages of the

Northern Caucasus as the Germans retreated at the beginning of the year, and the mass killings of thousands of Jews throughout their occupation of the territory. Tolstoy wrote:

> The Germans began to prepare for the massacre in the very first days of the occupation. They organised Jewish committees ... Old men, adolescents, invalids, scientists, doctors, old women who could hardly move their feet, were all driven to hard labour ... They were ordered to wear a yellow star on their breasts and forbidden to enter restaurants, stores or public places.

He went on to describe how they were then gathered together and placed on a train. The train travelled to the outskirts of a place named Mineralnye Vody. There they were told to leave the carriages, stripped of their belongings and their clothes, force marched toward an anti-tank ditch and there shot, all 2,000 of them. That same night, a further 500 Jews and some 1,500 children were taken to the same place and also shot, and this continued for several days. According to Tolstoy, after the German retreat, Russian excavations discovered in excess of 6,000 bodies. This makes sobering reading today with all we now know of the Holocaust; in 1943 it must have had an enormous impact on people previously unaware of such barbaric acts. For many it must have reinforced the view that this conflict, unlike the First World War, was one that had to be prosecuted until victory was absolute.

But there was still a long way to go and an awful lot of battles to be won. The news coming from the war was still largely positive. A new bomber airfield was opened at Desborough. Double summertime ended, with clocks going back one hour. A row erupted around the county with regard to shops opening on a Sunday. Strict adherence to the law meant they could not, but many had done so. The world had changed since the start of the war, and many people, particularly women, were working much longer hours. Sunday opening was seen by the retail trade as essential to the war effort. Up until September 1943, the county council had, in effect, turned a blind eye. But then they suddenly began to demand the law be obeyed. It was a row that rumbled on for the rest of the year, and was never satisfactorily resolved. All this discontent

The remains of a military building as it looks today at Polebrook.

was pushed to one side with the arrival of the Movietone News cameras in Kettering. Crowds gathered and streets were lined with an eager public as the cameras rolled to film the march past of 150 American 'coloured soldiers'. Marching to a 'swing drill', which had never been seen before, the soldiers chanted a marching song and moved to a rhythmic beat unlike anything that had been seen in the British Army. The film, essentially a welcome to the Americans, was shown in cinemas all across the county later in the year and proved a big success, particularly the marching chant, which those watching in 1943 were totally unfamiliar with.

Whilst all this was going on, there was one particular American causing quite a stir and catching a fair amount of press interest. During the summer, Hollywood superstar Clark Gable arrived in the small village of Polebrook. World famous for his part in films like *Mutiny on the Bounty*, *It Happened One Night*, *China Seas* and, of course, for uttering the most famous lines in cinema history – 'Frankly, my dear, I don't give a damn' – as Rhett Butler, playing opposite Vivien Leigh and Leslie Howard in *Gone with The Wind*. Joining the American Airforce after the death of his equally famous wife, Carole Lombard, in 1942, he had arrived in England as a first lieutenant. Promoted to captain, he flew in to Polebrook air base to make a film, *Combat America*, intended to be used as a recruitment aid to increase volunteers into the American armed forces. A familiar figure around the village and in nearby Oundle,

HIGH STREET, KETTERING.

Kettering High Street during the war years.

he toured all the American bases across the county during his stay and flew on five combat missions before returning to the States at the end of the summer.

Not that Northamptonshire's cattle farmers paid much attention to his visits. They were struggling by early autumn with an outbreak of anthrax, trying to keep it contained where it had broken out in a herd at Thrapston. According to the National Farmers' Union, by early September twenty cows and a horse had died of the infection. All the infected animals were cremated in pits dug on nearby land, and the remaining herds, including dairy cows, vaccinated against the disease. Movement of stock around designated farms had been stopped, and the worry of the infection spreading beyond the east side of the county quickly eased.

Whilst the situation was being handled by the police and various agricultural experts, the county's public health committee announced the decision by Northamptonshire County Council to try to prevent the spread of a very human disease, tuberculosis. According to the doctors, it tended to attack those aged between 10–40, cost the country as a whole £4.5 million annually and destroyed the ability of many to work. The authorities decided to implement, across the whole county, a mass radiography programme. The intention was to catch the disease in its early stages, hopefully treat it successfully and eventually eradicate it completely. To help those found to be infected and forced to stop work, the government agreed a financial grant, supplemented by the county council where necessary, to help alleviate any poverty. It was a sensible approach and, as time went on, certainly proved effective, though truly effective treatment did not arrive until 1946 with the discovery of streptomycin.

News from the war throughout the end of summer and early autumn continued to reinforce the hope that the war in Europe was nearing its end. Sicily had fallen by mid-August and Montgomery's Eighth Army had been diverted toward Italy, where it landed on 3 September near Calabria. That caused the Italian government to renege on its German alliance and forced a surrender five days later. Allied troops landed at Salerno twenty-four hours later to begin a full-scale invasion of the Italian mainland, although that proved to be a far more difficult task than originally believed. Hitler instructed his forces to take over Rome and begin building lines of defence the Italian army had failed to carry out. He also insisted Mussolini be rescued from his imprisonment, which was carried out by German forces before the Allies could reach him. The Italian dictator was then flown to Hitler's headquarters at Rastenburg in East Prussia. Left with little choice, the Italian government he left behind made a more rational decision and decided to join with the Allies a month later.

With these successes and the Russians having begun major offensives on the Eastern Front, Anthony Eden flew to Moscow. There he met with ministers from America, Russia and China to formally set in motion the proposal Churchill and Roosevelt had discussed months earlier, the formulation of a world body that would maintain world peace after the war, the United Nations. The four signed a declaration to that effect, which was in turn ratified when Churchill, Roosevelt and Stalin met on 1 December in Tehran.

It was a key document that formed the basis upon which the United Nations today operates out of New York, though one that carried little weight at the time it was conceived. Then there was still a very strong Germany to overcome, something Bomber Command was all too well aware of, as were the people of Northamptonshire.

Castle Ashby, used extensively by the military during the war years.

Throughout the year, local newspapers constantly headlined the success of the RAF's attacks on those German towns and cities that had formed Bomber Command's strategy at the start of the year. But by the winter only one target city was front page most days: Berlin. Bomber Command's Arthur Harris suggested to Churchill that a combined operation, British and American, could destroy the German capital and shorten the war. Churchill was supportive. The Americans were not, understandably so in view of the high losses they had sustained in both aircraft and crew throughout the summer. Undeterred, Harris decided to proceed with his plan, and between November and Christmas launched sixteen major air attacks on the German capital. Losses were very heavy and the destruction wrought on the city huge. On the night of 2 December alone, as reported by the *Northamptonshire Evening Telegraph*, the RAF lost forty-one aircraft and the raids did not really achieve their objective.

Closer to home, the effect of this bombing strategy was felt by the villagers of Deenethorpe when an American Flying Fortress bomber, carrying a 6,000lb bomb load, exploded on the edge of the village. Fortunately for all those living there, the crew managed to alert the residents and get everyone out of their homes before the explosion. Damage was extensive, with every house affected, some more extensively than others. The homeless were housed in the rectory at nearby Deene, the other householders joining workmen from the surrounding villages to make running repairs to homes that could be made habitable again. Prompt action by the air crew had doubtless saved lives. The incident made everyone famous for a day: the BBC arrived shortly afterwards to make a radio programme for broadcast to North Africa and Canada. American newsreel cameras followed on to film the destruction and carried out interviews with those who had been affected.

Fortunately for all concerned, most of the houses were back to normal by Christmas and life returned to the usual routines. Elsewhere across the county, the WVS was organizing work of a different kind. In co-ordination with the British Red Cross, members were involved in a number of winter projects. Groups were set up to make toys for children in nurseries and hospitals. Others were repairing camouflage nets or, along with the YMCA, involved in collecting whatever vegetables were available, loading them into sacks and delivering them to Grimsby. The Vegetables for Minesweepers scheme ran throughout December, providing vegetables to the Royal Navy. Appeals for the Red Cross, particularly for the provision of supplies to be sent to prisoners of war, were launched in all parts of Northamptonshire during late November and early December. All such projects were extremely well supported, funds generally being raised through the running of fetes and fairs. According to many who survived as prisoners, receiving these parcels was often a life-saver, as countries operating prison camps often struggled to feed the men they held in captivity as the war progressed.

These were not the only cases in need. We tend to believe that the concept of workhouses died out with the Victorians; it did not. What did was the name, but workhouses were renamed Public Assistance Institutions or turned into hospitals such as St Edmunds in Northampton and Park Hospital in Kettering. Managing the funds and supporting the people in need, by the time war started, were the Guardian Committees. These committees, based in Northampton, Daventry, Kettering, Wellingborough, Brixworth and Towcester, provided food, income or both. In December 1943, after a debate that had raged for months, it was finally decided to provide, as well as basic subsistence, 2s. (10p) a week spending money to all those aged over 65, and a Christmas-only extra to those married of 4s. (20p), with 2s. and 6d. (12½p) to singles and an extra 1s. and 6d. (7½p) for any child. Poverty had clearly not been entirely eradicated.

However, across the county on Christmas Day, unlike the previous four Christmases, there was a mood of optimism, with news from every front apparently positive. So the celebrations this time around were less muted: hospitals held concerts, American servicemen visited the children and in places played the role of Santa, churches were full and hopes were high for an end to the war.

A further cause of optimism was the news that the mighty German battleship *Scharnhorst* had at last been cornered by the Royal Navy and, after a long sea battle with HMS *Duke of York* and her escorts, sunk off Norway's North Cape on Boxing Day.

CHAPTER SIX

1944
Hitting Back

For most people living in Northamptonshire at the start of 1944, it wasn't just the war causing issues of concern. Optimism was high that the end was in sight, buoyed by the fact that there had been an influx of American soldiers across southern England, the inference being that an Allied attack on German-occupied France was now inevitable. However, on a more mundane level, the county council, supported by other councils around the county, reported that 1943 had been a very dry year. Despite it being the middle of winter, many reservoirs were two-thirds empty. According to reports from the water board, the second great drought in ten years had begun. Back in 1934, water had been severely rationed, with no supplies at all for certain periods every day. What was intended this time was that warnings alone would be sufficient to ensure every house and every business across Northamptonshire would reduce its consumption significantly. The message was widely publicized that water was only to be used for drinking, and for no other purpose. The drought did eventually resolve itself, but for much of the early part of 1944 it remained a serious issue, particularly for the military.

By this time the USAAF had an extremely strong presence around the county. Spanhoe, some 6 miles outside Uppingham, was the latest airfield to be taken over by the Americans. The 315th Troop Carrier Group moved in from the beginning of January, the first aircraft arriving on site on 7 February. By this time aircraft in the skies above Northamptonshire were a common sight, but with it often came tragedy. A Wellington bomber crash landed into woodland around Geddington on 21 January, killing three crew. Three days later, at Braybrooke, a second Wellington hit the ground, killing three more crew members. As a result, in rural areas around the county there was a growing acceptance by people of the dangers present, not only to themselves, but the men who flew the aircraft they had grown used to seeing above their heads. There was a particular curiosity from locals about the Americans who manned many of the airfields and did much of the daylight flying. Equally curious, local newspapers sent reporters out to meet these visitors from the other side of the world, as eager as the Northants public to know more about them. What they found was an air force much like the RAF, perhaps the exception being in the way the Americans were able to supply their airbases. What had disappeared from the British diet was more readily available to the American airmen: chocolate, sweets, bananas, sugar and so on, much of which the airmen tended to give away when they could. According to a report in the *Northamptonshire Evening Telegraph*, many of them also carried good luck charms, generally attached to a chain: 'Ivory horses, monkeys, a green-eyed cat, Chinese characters, a ring, a fragment of shell splinter, all were on show as infallible bringers of good luck … But overall, just like everyone else, they wanted to bring the war to an end.'

As did the Home Guard. Well-honed by this time into an effective fighting force, they had been agitating to be allowed to join the Regular Army in any future attack on Europe. All around the county, many of those young enough had expressed a desire to be allowed to fight when the time came; so much so that the question had been raised in Parliament, and, thankfully, been rejected. The Home Guard, it was decided, was exactly that, a fighting force that would stay at home. Even as the war began to turn in the Allies' favour, the prospect of German paratroopers landing around Britain was still a possibility. Perhaps it was a long shot by this stage of the war, but nevertheless it was not discounted.

Yet as ever, it was not always only the war, or those involved in it, that grabbed the headlines. In the middle of January, two goods trains – the Leicester-London train with nine wagons and a local train travelling between Wellingborough and Nuneaton – ran into each other just north of Kettering. The damage was extensive, with the Kettering to Leicester line closed for several hours. Fortunately there were no fatalities, the only injury being to a guard who sustained broken ribs.

Elsewhere, the effects of rationing were still being felt. Long queues formed outside shops, particularly for eggs, which were extremely difficult to obtain, as well as goods like biscuits, tinned tomatoes, tinned peas and sausages. Since the previous summer, no other items had been added to the rationed list, but those on it often proved elusive. Even shoes and boots were difficult to obtain, despite being rationed. A man could only buy one pair of boots or shoes every thirteen months, a woman one pair every eight months. In the main, as pointed out by Rushden's Boot Manufacturers' Association president John White at a well-attended meeting held in the town, even with these restrictions lifted, supply would be difficult to maintain. The industry needed more young people to enrol on the industry's technical training programmes and view it as a career with a serious future. Continuity of skilled labour, he told the audience, would be vital when the war ended. Manufacturers also needed the release of leather held in occupied countries as soon as could be allowed. Here he was addressing an issue caused by the Italian involvement in the war, which had restricted supplies of certain types of leather. But the war still had a long way to go.

Out in the Far East, it would last longer than the European war, and for many it had become something of a forgotten war. The 1st Battalion Northamptonshires were out in India, and for families back in Northampton that brought the conflict with the Japanese closer to home, with newspaper headlines perhaps having a bit more personal meaning. By the start of 1944, it had become clear after the fall of Burma that India was the next likely target for the Japanese army. The Northants were moved from their positions on India's North-West Frontier and in Ceylon to positions around the Kabaw Valley on the Burmese border. They were likely to be involved in meeting any Japanese advance, which made any news coming out of that area extremely important and powerfully relevant.

However, news was hard to obtain. Much of what was published came from the war nearer home. The Russians were advancing into Romania, the Allies were bogged down in central Italy around Monte Cassino, Allied troops were winning ground out in New Guinea, and the RAF and the American air force were now mounting regular 1,000 bomber raids over German cities. Patience was the order of the day, but as spring began even that was becoming stretched. Distraction came in the form of images of General Montgomery – Monty – in every newspaper calling on everyone to give money to the 'Salute the Soldier' campaign. This was another fundraising mechanism intended to augment what had gone before by invoking the spirit of Alamein, and was readily embraced, as in previous years, though this time perhaps with more fervour and belief. The nationwide campaign rolled out in London on 25 March.

Twenty-four hours before that launch, however, Northamptonshire was hit hard by news of a tragedy close to home. Whilst attempting a take-off from Chelveston Airfield in the early hours of the morning, an American B-17 Flying Fortress bomber crashed into buildings in the village of Yelden. The subsequent explosion caused huge devastation, blew out the church windows, killed all ten aircrew and a further eleven people asleep in their beds. Two of the victims were children, Keith and Monica Phillips; miraculously, their parents survived, but their bungalow did not. All that was left of the home was two stumps of brickwork, one at either end. It took fire fighters some two hours to extinguish the flames and avoid any further explosions. The

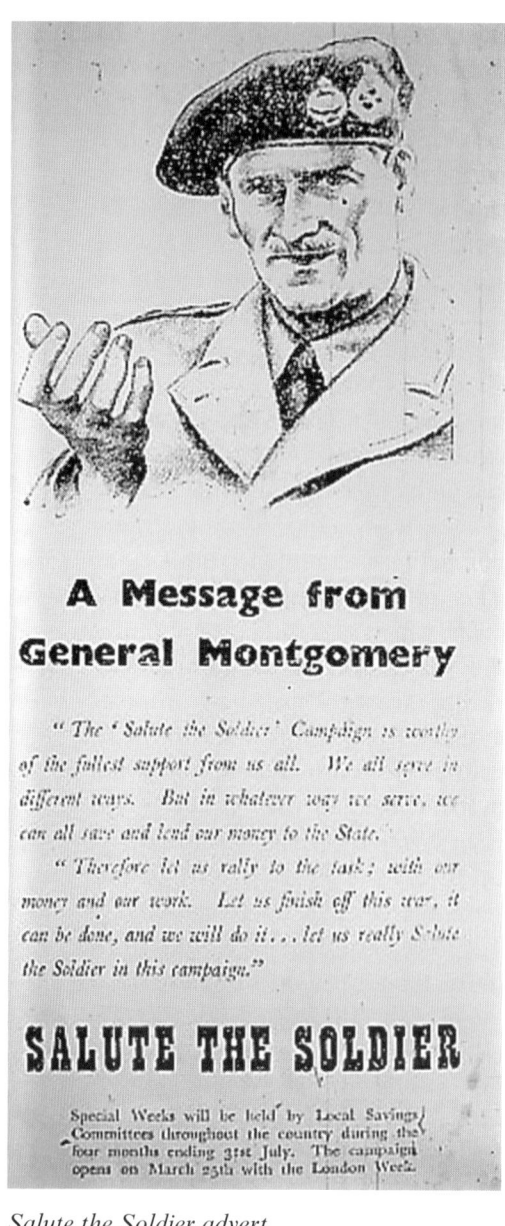

Salute the Soldier advert.

names of those who were killed can be seen today in the village church.

Wartime flying clearly often came at a cost. It was also a necessity, and the bravery of those who carried out the various missions was highlighted in local newspapers when it was announced that an award for bravery had been received by a Raunds airman. Acting Flight Lieutenant Cyril Spriggs had carried out ten bombing missions over Berlin, as well as an undefined number over various other well-defended targets. He was awarded the Distinguished Flying Cross (DFC) for gallantry, along with others of RAF No 57 Squadron. At around the same time, news was also released of a Victoria Cross awarded to the Northamptonshire Regiment's Lieutenant Alec Horwood for outstanding bravery in a three-day action against the Japanese at Kyauchaw, Burma, from 18-20 January.

This second award turned attention back to the threat by the Japanese toward India and the men of the Northants (known as the Steelbacks, a nickname dating back to the Peninsular War in the early nineteenth century) helping to hold the defensive line. The first real news of their involvement in the fighting came as the Japanese launched attacks on the Burmese border on 6 April. A short article published by the *Northampton Evening Telegraph* told of heavy fighting in the Kabaw Valley and of the Northamptonshires' attempt, in advance of the Allied forces there, to prevent the Japanese capturing the road to Imphal. The newspaper gave no further details, but we know now that the fighting there and later at Imphal was exceptionally fierce and savage. Imphal was a battle that raged for some three months, the Allies at one stage being completely surrounded and suffering an incredibly high loss of life, but they held on. The Japanese were eventually forced to retreat, ending their hopes of invading India. The Northants played a vital part in inflicting on the Japanese Imperial Army its first defeat, marking an end to their advances in the Far East. It was a key turning point of the jungle war.

Back home, the drought that had caused so much consternation at the start of the year had eased, but the water supply across the whole county was highlighted as being inadequate. With a view to the future, a study had been undertaken by Westminster to ascertain just what the problems were and how they could be alleviated by effective planning. It was found that Northampton, Wellingborough, Daventry and Kettering were the key problem areas, which would, in part, be relieved by the construction of a reservoir at Pitsford and a second one accessing the River Ise around Kettering. Further investment was then required to allow water supplies to be delivered around the county from whatever source was available, by increasing the mains supply and access to it. Daventry was cited as a particular problem area in need of investment because of its reliance on wells scattered around the villages. The report formed the basis for all future planning, most of the changes along with the investment coming after the war.

As all this was dissected and digested, and some of the reported findings were published county-wide for people to read and understand, news broke of the loss of Group Captain Percy Pickard. His wife, Dorothy, was well known in Northamptonshire, her family living in Kings Cliffe, while he was involved in the film *Target for Tonight*, a documentary made by the Ministry of Information in which real people played themselves (using a pseudonym). The film showed how a night-time bombing raid over Germany was carried out, and featured a Wellington bomber targeting Kiel. Percy Pickard played the part of Squadron Leader Dickson, captain of 'F for Freddy', using real-time film footage. It received widespread acclaim and a special Academy Award for best documentary. Twenty-eight-year-old Pickard, the first RAF officer to be awarded the DSO (Distinguished Service Order) and two bars, had received the DFC in 1940. An exceptionally brave pilot, he flew missions over occupied France to supply agents of the SOE (Special Operations Executive) and took part in various bombing missions over Europe. Initially reported missing, his death was not confirmed until September. It transpired after the war that he had been killed after flying a Mosquito fighter-bomber in a secret mission to bomb the prison and Gestapo headquarters in Amiens, northern France.

Meanwhile, despite the drought and the news coming in from the war, life went on as normal around Northamptonshire. Double summer time was back after the clocks had gone on by one hour at the start of April, and the Cobblers beat Notts County 4-1. There had been a successful flag day held for all those at sea, and across the county, councils were looking at relaxing the need for

Fire Watchers as bombing right across the country, though still happening, had lessened somewhat. It was therefore felt that with longer daylight hours and most air raids restricted to the hours of darkness, there was no need for men and women involved in doing the job to be active before 10 pm. The original proposal came from Kettering. The argument given was that for many of those volunteering it had become an onerous duty, and a relaxation of the hours would be beneficial to all. There was a degree of support across the region, and as time went on strict vigilance became less necessary.

What was likely to become very necessary was new houses, and in early May, Kettering launched an exhibition at the Alfred East Art Gallery on the future of housebuilding. It was intended that the exhibition visit other towns around the county to show new ideas in the construction industry, centred around pre-fabricated housing. In parts of Britain bombing had caused extensive damage and generated a demand for new homes that were cheap and easy to construct. In other areas, Northamptonshire being an example, the existing housing stock was of poor quality. Most newly married couples were unable to afford or find a home for themselves, and were forced to either live with parents or rent rooms. The homes that were available were, in most instances, built pre-1914. It was hoped the exhibition would generate public support for an idea that could solve a problem, particularly in the short-term. Hundreds went to see just what pre-fabrication was all about, though there seems little evidence it ever found real favour in the county.

Whilst people were looking at the possible future, the Americans took over Harrington Airfield near Rothwell, a significant and at the time secret installation. The 801st Provisional Bomber Group that moved in flew modified B-24 Liberator bombers, which were painted black. Operating under their code name of 'The Carpetbaggers', they worked closely with another essentially secret squadron, the RAF's Moon Squadron, flying out of Tempsford, and were responsible for supplying arms, ammunition, supplies and occasionally secret agents or saboteurs (known as Joes) into occupied Europe.

A few weeks later, in early May, members of the press and representatives of the American forces stationed in Britain congregated outside Cransley's church, along with troops from

Cransley Church today.

Czechoslovakia and Britain, to attend a ceremonial unveiling. The Americans, as a thank-you for the courtesy and kindness extended toward them, had raised money to create a stained-glass window, which they gifted to the little church. It depicted President Roosevelt and Prime Minister Churchill on the deck of a battleship, agreeing to the formulation of the Atlantic Charter, with the symbolic image of two soldiers, one British and the other American, shaking hands beneath the tree of life. The unveiling, carried out by Lance Corporal Francis Stapleton, whose wife was first soprano in the church choir, and Private (first class) Bernard Jackson of Mississippi, took place before a packed congregation. It was, according to Colonel Henry A. Wingate, who gave an address at the end of the service, a fitting gift to the church, which had offered to arrange a Thanksgiving service for the American troops when they had first arrived in November 1942, something he felt strongly had helped welcome soldiers – many of whom had never left home before – to a country that was very different and very new to them. The vicar spoke some very apposite words when, after thanking them, he told the listening soldiers: 'You are about to share in the greatest battle of all time.' How right he was.

For many that battle had begun many months ago, but for the USAAF in Northamptonshire, May 1944 was a very bad month. Polebrook lost fifteen aircraft, Chelveston fourteen, Deenethorpe the same number and Grafton Underwood nine. The RAF also lost an undisclosed number of aircraft bombing Essen, and news had broken that British and American forces had made an amphibious landing at the Italian seaside resort of Anzio (Operation Shingle). Coupled with newspaper headlines and cinema newsreels that confirmed the troop build-up around the country, to most locals, despite the losses, the war effort had moved up a gear.

There were also other contributory factors. Trains continually ran at capacity and late. Rail freight, which was being moved through the county in ever-increasing amounts, caused unprecedented delays to rail passenger services. On the roads, increased levels of military traffic, coupled with a noticeable increase in military activity and more troop movements than normal, snarled up traffic and made movement around the county difficult. The expectation of something big about to happen had grown expeditiously.

94 NORTHAMPTONSHIRE AT WAR 1939–45

This is not surprising when documents released after the war revealed the Americans by this time had shipped in some 50,000 tanks, 450,000 tons of ammunition and around 1.5 million men. This vast army, alongside the Canadian, Free French, Polish, Belgian, Dutch, Norwegian, Czech and some 1.7 million British troops were scattered all around southern counties of England. Above them, flying almost daily throughout May, RAF Lancaster bombers and American B-17s headed out to destroy the French railway system and Hitler's vaunted Atlantic Wall, which stretched from Norway to the Spanish frontier.

At Spanhoe airfield, as part of this build up, American paratroopers began arriving on 3 June, although their presence was never publicly acknowledged. A day later, American troops entered Rome, and on 5 June those same paratroopers left Spanhoe on board forty-seven aircraft at precisely 10.50 pm, their destination Sainte Mere Eglise in Normandy, which became the first French town to be liberated. The long-awaited D-Day had finally arrived. Many people awoke to the familiar sound of heavy bombers flying across

General Montgomery, General Eisenhower and Sir Arthur Tedder, who was Deputy Supreme Commander under Eisenhower for the D-Day landings.

the county early the following morning as they headed for northern France and the beaches around Normandy. Confirmation coming later that day with a radio broadcast from the BBC informing listeners that Allied troops had begun landing on the Normandy coast. As they later discovered, it was the largest amphibious assault ever mounted, involving approximately 7,000 ships, some 11,000 aircraft and around 130,000 Allied troops landing at a number of targeted beaches, along with a further 23,400 troops dropped by parachute or glider behind German lines. The Northamptonshires were also involved, taking part in the capture of Le Havre and the following battle for Caen. For many households, the news, uplifting as it was, also held a deal of personal involvement.

The next few days were obviously dominated by progress across the Channel, and everyday life was difficult to maintain with any sense of normality. But the war on a local level was never far away. Six days after the invasion, a fragmentation bomb exploded at Deenethorpe, killing six people. On the following day, the first of what would become a devastating new German weapon, the V-1 rocket, began appearing over southern England. Despite the Allied breakthroughs in France and the apparent retreat of German armies on all fronts, Hitler had succeeded in developing the first ballistic missile and successfully deployed it against Britain. Within a week, the 'doodlebugs', as they became known, had killed around 800 civilians and wounded over 2,500. Indiscriminate, essentially untargeted and without warning, these missiles could fall anywhere at any time. It put life on the edge, and Northamptonshire was not out of range.

Toward the end of June, newspaper headlines were following the Allies through northern France and highlighted the RAF and American bomber successes over Germany. There was a hugely effective 1,000 bomber raid over Berlin, this time supported by 1,200 fighters. More such raids were to follow. The Russians were continuing to advance in the East, the Americans had made a breakthrough in the Philippines and the Japanese, after their defeat at Imphal, also began losing ground all across the Pacific. Inevitably, on the home front at least, despite the V-1s, there was a growing sense that the war was reaching its end.

With optimism high, the king and queen, along with Princess Elizabeth, paid a visit to Chelveston Airfield to meet American

His Majesty the King

His Majesty King George VI.

ground crew – their second visit in two years to Northamptonshire. In 1943, they had been at Sears Shoe Company and the Gas Company, so were familiar faces in the county. A couple of weeks later, the first V-1 rocket hit Northamptonshire at Creaton, where it apparently fell in Turland's Orchard but was not reported because the War Office did not want the Germans to know how far it had travelled. It was not the only incident. A second rocket fell on 23 December, and there are reports of a third also hitting the county at around this time. We know now that these were not deliberately aimed at Northamptonshire and were more than likely just off target. Nevertheless, at the time they reminded people that Hitler was not yet defeated.

To that end, a second D-Day, Operation Dragoon, was carried out on 15–16 August when the Allies landed in southern France, which was still occupied by the Germans. A complete success, it forced the German army to retreat and Paris fell eleven days later. The battle for France continued for a few more days, but essentially the Allies had broken out of the Normandy bridgehead, captured the southern part of the country, liberated its capital and were about to storm the Siegfried Line and enter Germany.

With life in Northamptonshire now perhaps a little quieter than it had been, a request from London for ARP wardens to assist in their fight against the flying bombs, which were wreaking havoc across the capital, met with a huge response. A number of men from the county volunteered to give up their time to go and work in London and help wherever they could. Largely supported by local employers, particularly the shoe trade, businesses allowed their employees to go without incurring any financial penalties. It was a generous gesture by all concerned, with some 112 men travelling south, with more prepared to replace them when needed. Whilst this was ongoing, the Clothing Manufacturing Co-operative met in Kettering to address the pressing issue of clothes for Europe and the future necessity of supplying the various services with clothing when their men were eventually demobbed. As the Germans retreated toward their border, those left behind in previously occupied countries were without adequate clothing for the coming winter, essentially because of the lack of available labour within their communities and too few textile factories that had not been damaged or destroyed by bombing. Manufacturers here therefore decided to provide any surplus clothing sourced locally, particularly for children, and organize its despatch abroad when the war situation allowed.

The future of the Home Guard was also under discussion across Northamptonshire by midsummer, the argument being mounted, particularly by the national press, that it no longer served a purpose. Advances in Europe had put paid to any possible German invasion of the British mainland. But there was still a strong body of opinion that, whilst invasion by sea or air was now impossible, there was still the threat posed by Hitler's growing use of the V-1 rocket, and now the modified version, the V-2. These, it was argued, could carry gas or greater explosive charges than had been the case so far. Supporting the military and organizing the local population in the event of an attack was the Home Guard's key strength. Disbanding at this stage what was in effect a successful arm of local Civil Defence was simply too soon. It was a reasonably valid argument, and the Army tended to agree. It was therefore decided to maintain the force as it was, but reduce the day-to-day routines it had been accustomed to since 1940, with less of the guard duty and no more weekly parades.

It was not only the Home Guard that began to question their situation as the war seemed to move forward in a more positive way. Teachers also began to make greater demands. Across the county there were still thousands of evacuees, and with the rocket attacks still being made on London they were likely to stay beyond the end of the year. The county education committee became more vocal about the teaching posts still vacant and not likely to be filled for some considerable time. The problem was simply one of numbers, with class sizes in some areas of the county becoming too large for schools to cope with. Kettering, Wellingborough and Northampton particularly began to struggle, and wanted government assistance to bring more teachers into the county from other areas to help out until the situation could be resolved. They understood all too well that would probably not be until the war ended, and at this stage no-one knew when that would be.

The signs, however, were distinctly positive that peace was a little nearer when it was announced on 16 September that the total blackout was over, as was double summer time. Both had affected everyone's life for five years, but the purely wartime inventions were no longer seen as necessary. The exceptions were coastal areas in England, Scotland and Wales, where showing lights was still deemed to be dangerous. So across Northamptonshire, street lights were back on; not at full brightness, but certainly brighter than they had been since the start of the war. Car lighting, however, remained dimmed, with only bicycles allowed to show a full light.

However, a timely reminder that there was still a lot of fighting to be done, particularly in the Far East, came in a letter published by local newspapers from a Northamptonshire soldier fighting with the Chindits in Burma:

> You read of the Russian armies, the 1st, the 5th, the famous 8th Army locked in battle over a vast area – but they do know what's going on. They can see what they are doing, and that is a big thing, they can see. Out here it is quiet, uncanny, deathly stillness that keeps you on edge. Then suddenly hell breaks loose and you never know where it comes from. All you can see is an everlasting wall of green, of light and dark shadows, impenetrable to the eyes. There is no front here, the enemy is all around you.

The letter went on to describe the appalling conditions of jungle fighting and the lack of supplies. By this stage of the war, the Chindits had become more than a thorn in the side of the Japanese. Though little was published about it back in Britain, there had been heavy fighting in Burma during the summer months, and the Northamptonshires had been involved and would remain so into 1945. The letter at least began to tell a little of what it was like to fight in a jungle environment, and was for most a reminder that the war in the Far East was not going to be easy to resolve.

In Europe, the front line moved ever closer to Germany's western borders, while the air war had been diverted from bombing cities such as Hamburg and Berlin, to locating and destroying Germany's transport system, oil industry and other sources of power. There was also an urgent need to locate the secret weapons research centre at Peenemunde, where factories housed and developed the V-2 rocket, which was causing so much death and destruction across southern England. The attacks on Germany's infrastructure had an effect on their ability to continue the war, but just how effective in places like Berlin was not really known until articles began appearing in the local press from British soldiers returning to Northamptonshire after repatriation. One such story came from a corporal in the Northamptonshire Regiment who had been wounded in the desert war and captured in 1942. After being treated for wounds by the Italians and spending time in Italy, he had been transferred to a PoW camp in Germany at the end of 1943. He told the British press on his return home that the Germans were suffering from food deprivation: 'They make acorn coffee and mint tea and will do anything to get soap, cocoa, coffee, tea, and chocolate from prisoners.'

The prisoners' food arrived via the Red Cross parcel distribution, much of it being shipped into the camps from family and friends in Northamptonshire or through the proceeds of various fundraising activities. According to the corporal's account of life in the camp, these parcels supplemented the poor food supplied by their captors, which consisted mainly of swede soup. As other stories began to emerge, all telling a similar tale, it became obvious that there was widespread suffering among the German people, reinforcing the view that the Allies were now on top and the war reaching its climax.

For Northamptonshire shoppers, the suffering was far less severe. Indeed, on the food front there had been a positive change. More non-rationed items started to become available throughout the autumn, which in turn caused argument and debate as to how it should be distributed. There were meetings in Kettering and Northampton to discuss the idea of introducing a household card scheme, whereby every house would have access to these

Abington Street, Northampton, during the war.

items without having to queue outside various shops. This idea was roundly rejected, as the shop owners preferred a free-market approach, and people were used to queuing by this time. What was more significant was the government announcement that there would be extra rations allowed for the Christmas period on the foods that had been in short supply for almost six years.

Under the new proposals, all shops across Northamptonshire were to allow an extra ½lb of sweets to those aged between 6 months and 18 years. For adults there was to be an extra ½lb of margarine, access to extra supplies of dried fruit for cake-making, an increased number of turkeys for Christmas dinner, more in the meat ration, a distribution of oranges, dates and an extra 1oz of tea each week for those over 70 years old. In addition to all this, vast amounts of almonds and peanuts were to be distributed to all retail outlets. It was good news for all, and well received by the public. Supplies had been released because of increased imports after the effective defeat of the German U-boats, the liberation of countries that had been under German control and an agreement with the Americans that those servicemen based in Britain would not use some British food sources over Christmas.

What the American forces did have access to, and the rest of Northamptonshire did not, was Glenn Miller. He and his dance band had been doing the rounds of American bases throughout southern England in the lead up to D-Day, and in October they arrived in Kings Cliffe. It was a sell-out crowd. Some 2,500, mainly US forces, descended on the airfield to listen to the much-broadcast and widely publicized big band sound. Sadly, two months later, Miller was killed when his Norseman aircraft went down in the Channel. Exactly where has never been discovered, and neither has his body.

At this time, newspapers were full of little other than war news from the various front lines. British paratroops cornered at Arnhem, after their unsuccessful attempt at capturing the Rhine bridge there, had suffered heavy losses. The German battleship *Tirpitz* had been attacked by the RAF and sunk in Tromso Fjord in Norway. The Americans were still battering the Siegfried Line, while mass bombing continued all across Germany, and out in the Far East, the Philippines were being retaken.

In Britain, the Home Guard was back in the news as winter began to set in. After all the debate throughout the summer, which had resulted in a partial reduction in the duties it carried out, it was decided to reverse that decision and put drills and parades back on the agenda. In Northampton, the Minister of Education, Rab Butler, announced the need for women employed in war work to be allowed to train for the teaching profession. This was a definite boost for women looking to build careers, and, according to reports, one that had been widely supported across the county. There was also a call for more people to join the county's renamed Royal Observer Corps, which was still operating all across the county but with a depleted force. The appeal was made because at this stage of the war there was a growing belief that their work was no longer a necessity. But of course it was. More aircraft were in the air over the county than at any other stage of the war. The corps was often the first to identify a bomber in difficulties and alert the relevant airfield. With so many bombing missions being carried out since the Normandy landings, and many of those involving aircraft flying from a Northamptonshire base, it's easy to see why there was still such a need.

For those at home with men fighting in northern France there also came news, though not necessarily good, of the Northamptonshire Yeomanry. As part of 33 Armoured Brigade, they had landed on the Normandy beaches on 12 June. They had taken part in fierce fighting around Caen, where tank gunner Joe Ekins, in his Sherman tank, achieved the amazing feat of destroying four German Tiger tanks in a single action, killing German tank ace Michael Wittmann (credited with destroying 132 tanks) in the process, for which he never received official recognition. They were also heavily involved in the fighting around the River Odon and in what became known as the 'Falaise Pocket'. But casualties were high in all these actions, and when the *Evening Telegraph* ran the story, many local families were still uncertain about who had survived or become a casualty.

There was further concern in the middle of December when newspapers and radio broadcasts reported that the Germans had mounted a huge offensive along a 100-mile front in the Ardennes. Heavy fog allowed the Germans to advance almost unhindered as all Allied aircraft were grounded, not just those in France but all across Northamptonshire. The war that seemed to be in its last moves had suddenly been thrown into chaos, and the impetus passed back to the German army. In what was labelled the Battle of the Bulge, US forces bore the brunt of the sudden, unexpected attack, being forced into hasty retreat. For several days the fighting was fierce across the sector. Then the weather broke, the fog lifted and bombing could resume, helping halt the German advance. The Allies were back on track and by Christmas the offensive was all but over. The Allies were back in control, with the defeated Germans falling back to their border. The likes of Montgomery, drafted in to help secure the faltering Allied defence, and combative US General Patton had won the day. But for the rest of December, there would be no rest for the Allies as they tried to push on into Germany.

In Northamptonshire, Christmas celebrations were back on track. Despite the earlier government announcement on relaxing the ration quotas, there were still shortages, including of Christmas cards. Fewer materials available to make and print them meant supplies were much lower than in the past. Wines and spirits were in a similar position, and difficult to find anywhere in the county. What were readily available, and had initially been thought of as very difficult to source, were children's toys. Marks & Spencer in Northampton, Kettering and Wellingborough had warned of shortages, but by the week before the holiday they reported a significant upturn. Dolls, games, soft toys, books and wooden toys were all made available. As were the promised turkeys, though according to newspaper reports, not necessarily through the local butcher. All things considered, by the close of business on Christmas Eve shops across the county reported trade at the highest levels they had seen since 1939. Christmas 1944 was set to be a celebration with real hope for the future.

CHAPTER SEVEN

1945
Victory

The first day of January 1945 dawned with skies above Northamptonshire and much of the south of England full of aircraft, as RAF and USAAF bombers began the New Year with a massive bombing campaign across Germany. For over five hours the sound of aircraft engines either flying out or returning were a constant throughout the early hours and beyond. The targets were Germany's industrial areas, railway networks and fuel supply dumps. On the ground, as reported by local and national newspapers, fighting around the Christmas period had been extremely fierce. After the Ardennes offensive had ground to a halt, the Luftwaffe launched massive air attacks against the Allied airfields scattered across Belgium and France. The German army, unable to break through the Allied line before Christmas, mounted a second offensive an hour before midnight on New Year's Eve in Alsace in a bid to retake Strasbourg. Both attacks, despite causing huge casualties, failed. But as people across the county read their newspapers or listened to the radio after celebrating New Year, they would have realized the war still had some way to go.

So did the winter. Across the whole shire there had been nothing but severe frosts for some time. Coal was still in short supply and all households were struggling to keep a fire burning in the grate. Even parts of the river froze, to a depth strong enough to allow skaters to take advantage of the severe cold snap. Wellingborough residents were photographed by local newspapers enjoying themselves at various points around the town. But it was Corby that hit the headlines at the start of January, as the BBC descended on Stewarts and Lloyds, the company responsible for PLUTO, the laying of the pipeline beneath the Channel to provide fuel to the

Allied forces in France. They had been chosen to star in the now very popular *Works Wonders Programme*, the entertainment show broadcast from a works or factory that had run for much of the war and had visited Rushden back in 1942. The stars featured were the workers themselves. At the Corby works, the BBC featured Stewarts and Lloyds' own works band, the Little Brothers, two men who worked on the blast furnace, plus Nessie Paterson, a singer employed in the typing pool, a member of Corby's Home Guard who was to be an impressionist for the day and Mildred Mount, a soloist from Kettering. The show was a huge success and gave everyone who wanted it the opportunity to have their chance in the spotlight.

Elsewhere, Corby housing was grabbing the headlines. It was decided just before the Christmas holiday that once the war had ended, a building programme would begin. The initial phase was to build at least 450 homes, a mix of two, three, four and five bedroom houses along with a number of temporary bungalows. The debate had already taken place about the viability of building pre-fab houses in the county, and after the Kettering exhibition there were further meetings in council chambers across the shire. The results of all that discourse were plans being put forward by various towns about their own housing hopes in a future, peaceful Britain. Only Weston Favell, at this stage, was selected as an area where pre-fab housing would work well. The Corby plan was for permanent, good quality homes, and not as a replacement for poor housing already in existence but as an addition. The plans were readily accepted and a timetable of around three years set for construction.

For those who would eventually return from the war it was a necessity, and the need for change was clearly in the air. For many families around the county, though, this was no more than a side issue. Bringing the troops home was obviously their key concern. Just after the start of the year, news broke that men who had taken part in the D-Day landings were being released on leave. The first groups had already arrived in London, where special trains were being laid on to ferry them to various parts of the country and their waiting families. All the trains were staffed by NAAFI (Navy, Army and Air Force Institutes) girls, who would act as hostesses, according to the *Northamptonshire*

Evening Telegraph. Canteens were set up at the various railway stations to provide hot food when the men arrived, though each travelling soldier was given a haversack containing, a ration of Cornish pasty, jam roll and cheese sandwiches before he left the transit camp in Belgium; no doubt welcome on what would be a long journey back to Britain. The first returnees arrived back in Northamptonshire late on 2 January, exhausted after some forty-eight hours' travel but eager to see families they had not seen since before the Normandy landings.

One thing they would not be short of once back home was entertainment. The cinemas had been full since Christmas. Audiences, spoiled for choice, were queuing every night to see the likes of Irene Dunne starring in *The White Cliffs of Dover*, Lon Chaney in *Of Mice and Men* and Don Ameche and Carmen Miranda in *Greenwich Village*. Alternatively, there was the Northampton Repertory Company's *The Scarlet Pimpernel* or the musical cabaret at Kettering's Savoy Theatre. There were no air raid sirens, no blackouts and no signs of the war they had left behind, except perhaps for the newsreel programmes and the sounds of bombers overhead. The RAF hit Hanover as part of another 1,000 bomber raid in the early hours of 6 January, causing so much devastation that the glow of the burning city could be seen for 200 miles. In the Far East, the US Pacific Fleet attacked Formosa and Okinawa, destroying over 100 Japanese aircraft and sinking or damaging around ninety-five ships, whilst on the Eastern Front, the Russian army attacked Warsaw and pushed the Germans back towards Berlin.

By mid-January, with the D-Day leave over and the soldiers returned to the front, Northamptonshire decided to begin using German prisoners of war on the county's farms, where labour was still in short supply. Key areas were those farmers trying to bring in the sugar beet crop. Lifting the crop and transporting it to the sugar beet factory in Peterborough had to be completed by 22 January. Weather conditions had been poor, which in turn made lifting the crop difficult. But for a fair number of farms, particularly in east of the county – Kettering, Deenethorpe, Weldon and Rushden – labour had also become an issue because lifting was pushed to later than was the norm. Using the prisoners therefore made significant sense, and for some they had saved the crop.

Any later and the beet would definitely have stayed in the ground, as heavy snow began to blanket the county by the third week of January. Some villages were cut off completely, sledges being used in Raunds and one or two other places to deliver coke to homes that had exhausted their coal supplies. The Royal Mail service was severely curtailed, with deliveries delayed, vans struggling to get mail and parcels to railway stations to meet mail trains, and gangs of platelayers being used by the railways to keep crossings and points clear from snow and ice. The biggest problem, snow aside, was illness. Hundreds succumbed to colds and infections, with some businesses finding staffing levels reduced by a third as the worst winter conditions for over twenty years began to bite. Prisoners of war were called out again in places to help clear snow from some of the county's main roads. In parts of the county, people had to dig their way through several feet of snow to get to shops and homes, whilst Corby had to call out snow ploughs.

By early February the snow had disappeared and life returned to normal. With spring in sight, attention began to turn toward the local supply of food. There were still some food stuffs in short supply and rationing, according to the government, was set to continue for the next few years. Concerns were raised about the lack of supply to the butchery trade of poultry and rabbits. At the start of the war, these were relatively freely available, as Northamptonshire was, in the main, a rural county. But through 1944 and into the New Year, it became evident that supply had fallen significantly, except on the 'black market'. Butchers complained that for many the poultry supply to the trade had simply dried up. The county's Food Executive Officer disagreed. According to their office, it was simply because most of the trade had gone into the central towns of Northampton and Wellingborough, where prices were roughly a penny a pound more expensive. The trade members were not convinced, arguing that the likes of Corby, which had twenty-one retail outlets licensed to sell both poultry and rabbits, had seen none for years. Yet both could still be bought by local people, rabbits selling for 5s. (25p) a pair. What had happened over the past year or so, as far as the poultry trade was concerned, was that poultry had been bought by local people claiming they were intending to keep them. These birds had then been slaughtered and sold on to friends and neighbours, without the trade ever being involved, depriving the market but maintaining the supply chain, albeit illegally.

Of even more importance was the growth in home-grown produce. At the annual general meeting of the Northants County Allotment Federation, it was clear the Dig For Victory campaign had caused the rise in public interest across Northamptonshire. Some eighty-five associations, with around 32,000 allotments, were represented by this stage of the war, only Oxfordshire being able to boast more. Seeds supplied from America early in the war had helped boost crop yields, and councils willing to give up land – only temporarily in many cases – had allowed the allotment industry to flourish. This had ensured a constant supply of vegetables, which were never rationed, and at this juncture of the war had begun to create a surplus. But as the federation told its members, with the end of the war in sight, these numbers would begin to decline. Land currently in use by many of its members was about to be reclaimed by the councils that had loaned it, in order that the future housing needs of the county could be met. The campaign had been an unmitigated success, but could no longer be maintained.

Change was clearly in the air as the county began to embrace the fact that the war was moving to its now inevitable conclusion. In Wellingborough, the Red Cross shop that had raised some £4,441 since its opening in 1940 was closing down. Run by a volunteer staff, mainly women, it had sold a huge variety of items, many home-made, and helped provide vital food supplies to prisoners of war held around Europe. Parcels were to continue in the short-term, but the shop, which operated on a rent-free basis and had become a familiar feature of the High Street, was no longer required. Neither was the British Restaurant based in Wellingborough. This was set up at the start of the war to provide hot meals to those working in the nearby industries. Organized by the local council, with all the meals supplied from kitchens in Earls Barton, it had been a huge success, providing some 300 meals each week, but had become difficult to maintain.

Elsewhere, a call went out again for volunteers to register their names to join one of the farming camps which were to be set up in June, as they had in previous years, to create a labour army to help with summer harvesting. According to the Agricultural

Committee, between 6,000–7,000 people would be needed this time around, with the volunteers paid 1s. (5p) an hour. The camps were in the same locations as before, along with new additions in Great Harrowden, Warmington, Hollowell and Farthinghoe.

But there was still a war to be won. In the air, the RAF and USAAF jointly bombed and destroyed Dresden in a huge firestorm. The Russians had captured Budapest and were approaching Berlin, and Winston Churchill, Joseph Stalin and Franklin D. Roosevelt met secretly at Yalta to discuss the reorganization of Europe after Hitler had been defeated. In the Far East, the Japanese were forced into retreat again at the Irrawaddy River and the Allied advance to recapture Burma began.

But these huge gains being made on all the key fronts also created a unique problem for the Allies: prisoners of war. In the House of Commons, Foreign Secretary Anthony Eden told MPs that as a result of Allied success the German infrastructure was breaking down and prisoners were being marched across the country without adequate food supplies due to disruption by British and US bombing. The Red Cross managed to get an agreement from the Germans that limited supplies of food parcels would be placed outside, or near to, PoW camps, and had organized a 100-lorry convoy to carry food from Switzerland into the German heartland. Unfortunately, the convoy was still on the Swiss border, unable to proceed and unlikely to do so until there was a lull in the fighting. That lull was not likely to happen soon. As Eden told parliament, and was reported in the local and

The 'big four', the Allied supreme commanders Winston Churchill, Franklin D. Roosevelt, Joseph Stalin and Chiang Kai-shek.

national press, money had been made available to the Red Cross to ensure, as best they could, that British prisoners were adequately protected whilst the war moved toward its climax.

And that denouement was not far away. By 7 March, the US First Army had crossed the Rhine over the railway bridge at Remagen. Two days later, Tokyo was bombed again, and out in the Pacific the Americans announced that they had finally secured Iwo Jima from the Japanese after four weeks of hard fighting. Berlin bore the brunt of further Allied bombing raids. Mosquito aircraft dropped 4,000lb bombs on the German capital, whilst the US heavy bombers targeted the vital railway yards at Kassel, Hagen and Siegen.

The local mood was lifted by news that the Steelbacks (Northamptonshire Regiment) were featured in a film showing at Northampton's Savoy Theatre called *Blighty Calling*. Featuring seventeen soldiers – one each from Rushden, Bugbrooke and Finedon and fourteen from Northampton – the short twelve-minute film (part of a series of films, some of which still survive) depicted serving soldiers in the Far East sending messages home to their families. A morale booster for the troops who formed what had become known as the forgotten army, it also provided a real lift for families in Northamptonshire, starved of news coming out of the Burmese jungle. Their war had not received the coverage given to those fighting across Europe, and the Northamptonshires were about to be launched, alongside the Indian army, at the Japanese as the Allies began their advance through Burma toward Mandalay. A brief mention was made of this in local newspapers in early March, but far more was made of the American advance across the lower Rhine in support of Operation Varsity, an airborne attack by 40,000 paratroopers on Germany itself.

Back in Northamptonshire, it was announced that major investment was to be made in housing at Duston on the outskirts of Northampton. The approved plan was to build 1,100 new homes and attract some 4,500 new families to the area. Other plans covering much of the county were also being discussed, the most contentious being the plan by the government to build on Northampton's racecourse. It came to light under the government's Requisition Land and Works Bill that the course was at risk, something not foreseen when the War Office had seized control of the land in 1939. A major campaign was launched to stop the prospect of any building taking place on the racecourse site and returning it to the wide open space that had been enjoyed by locals for some seventy years (a fight that was successful).

As March drew to a close, Mandalay finally fell to the Allies and the last ever V-1 and V-2 rockets fell on Britain. British Timken, which had opened a factory in Northampton after its base in the Midlands was made less safe by German bombing, had decided to stay. Manufacturers of roller bearings used in the manufacture of cars, lorries and aeroplanes, it had been guaranteed work by the Board of Trade. The plan was to create around 1,000 new jobs between 1945 and 1946 and work closely with Northampton's College of Technology to provide the necessary skills for its engineering workforce. For Northampton, it would mean an industrial diversification, as the town was essentially based around the shoe industry. Timken, it was hoped, would begin to introduce new industrial practices and possibly bring in other industrial businesses. Daventry also announced it was looking closely at how it could bring a similar type of industrial change to the town. With some 385 men and women on active service, there was apparently a strong feeling that existing industries around the town would be insufficient when they returned to the jobs market. Failure to do so, according to the council and the local branch of the British Legion, would result in high unemployment and a move by families away from the town in search of work elsewhere. This was a view no doubt held in a number of towns around the county, particularly when much of the working population was totally dependent on the shoe industry continuing to be both competitive and successful. John White, who had given the site for Higham's Town Hall, was much lauded at this time after it was announced that so far in the war his factories in Higham Ferrers and Rushden had manufactured some 8 million pairs of service footwear. The question asked by councils looking to the future was whether it could remain as successful after the war?

Whilst that question was being posed and discussed, a new Allied offensive was launched in Italy. Mussolini had been back in the headlines after resurfacing in the north of the country, from where it was reported he had reviewed the crack Italian Bersaglieri Regiment. With the war in Italy at a virtual standstill after the battles around Monte Cassino and the failure to break the deadlock at Anzio, German forces had fallen back to defend what became known as the Gustav Line. To break the deadlock, the Allies ordered a massive aerial bombardment aimed at breaking the Germans' lines of communication, which in turn would cut off their supply line and force them to retreat. Meanwhile, in Germany itself, the Americans had entered Cologne, or what was left of it after all the bombing it had sustained, and the Russians had edged ever nearer to Berlin. Events suddenly began to develop very quickly.

As the German armies were pushed relentlessly back toward their capital, the Allies began to uncover a horror that had been so carefully hidden away: the concentration camps. The first camp to hit the headlines was Buchenwald near Weimar, which was liberated by the American 6th Armoured Division on 11 April after it had received a Morse code message from the inmates, who used a hidden transmitter requesting help. What they found were thousands of emaciated men and women living in extreme conditions, many near death, most having been starved and beaten. The news of the discovery shocked the world. Worse would follow.

The following day, the death was announced of President Roosevelt. Vice President Harry S. Truman took over control of the country. Vienna fell to the advancing Russians and the British entered the second concentration camp to be liberated, Bergen-Belsen. Here they found around 60,000 gaunt, acutely ill, starving inmates who had received no food or water for several days, and about 13,000 dead lying in the open. The whole scene was recorded and later broadcast by the BBC, whose reporter Richard Dimbleby accompanied the troops. A few weeks later, a more personal account was published by local newspapers with a letter from a British officer to his parents in Olney describing the conditions discovered at Bergen-Belsen:

> Try to imagine walking along a mile of bodies, not able to tell whether they were dead or alive. The SS who did it are here to bury them, which they do all day long at the double. Men, women and children, naked or half naked are all mixed up and more like the lowest form of animal life imaginable. It was skilled, scientific torture.

We know today that over the duration of the war there were around 50,000 killed at the camp, some 10,000 of them dying in the first part of 1945 from diseases like typhus, typhoid, dysentery and tuberculosis. The British burned down the Bergen-Belsen camp once they had cleared it to stop the spread of disease. News was soon to follow of other camps – Auschwitz, Dachau and Sobibor, to name but three – but for many in Britain it would only be after the war that the true horror of these places began to surface.

Throughout April, it seemed every news story was about the consequences of the Allied advance and the collapse of the Third Reich. On 19 April, the Americans took Leipzig, and two days later the Allies in Italy captured Bologna. US and Russian forces finally met at Torgau on the River Elbe on 25 April. Three days after that, Mussolini was back in the headlines after being captured for a second time attempting to cross the Swiss frontier with his mistress Clara Petacci. This time there was no reprieve: both were shot dead by partisans, their bodies hung upside down from a metal girder above a service station in Milan. By the end of the month, news broke that Hitler and Eva Braun (whom he married just before his death) had committed suicide in his bunker in Berlin, a city by this time under constant bombardment from the air and on the ground as the Russians moved in to put an end to German resistance.

German forces still active in the city finally surrendered on 2 May. On the following day, British forces captured Hamburg, while in the Far East, Rangoon in Burma was taken. Two days later, German forces surrendered in Holland, north-west Germany and Denmark. The formal end to all hostilities in Europe followed, and VE (Victory in Europe) Day was declared on 8 May.

Celebrations across Northamptonshire had started at the beginning of May with the reintroduction of the May Day Queen for a number of villages where the tradition had been suspended since the outbreak of war. Kislingbury crowned the daughter of a previous May Day Queen who had presided at festivities at the end of the Great War. Crick resurrected the maypole, along with dancing to a well-played violin. Scaldwell crowned the daughter of a 7 Armoured Brigade serviceman, now held prisoner by the Japanese in Java, and then made a collection in support of PoWs not yet released, and so it went on all around the county. As news broke that the war was finally over and VE Day was official, churches rang their bells, people left their homes to fill the streets, cinemas and theatres spontaneously emptied, anyone in a uniform was hugged, kissed and thanked, and announcements were made that the shops would close for two days, as would schools. Even mail deliveries were stopped for twenty-four hours, along with the buses, while to help the festivities all pubs extended their opening hours until 11 pm. So began forty-eight hours of celebration.

Northampton Council authorized the spending of £100 on flags and bunting. Hospitals all across Northamptonshire were suddenly bedecked in Union Jacks, Stars and Stripes and the Russian hammer and sickle, and street parties sprang up all over Northampton and around the county. Daventry burnt an effigy of Hitler at the bottom of Ashworth Street, its arm outstretched in Nazi salute. Fireworks lit the night sky, victory parades in Northampton, Kettering and Wellingborough brought thousands out on to the streets, and parties went on long into the night.

The huge joyous outpouring took far longer than a couple of days to subside, but victory also meant change, and as the dust settled, the first of those changes had already begun. Children who had found a home in the county, the evacuee population that had been welcomed back in 1939, very quickly began to return to their own homes in London and the south of England. It was for many a sad time, particularly those families that had created strong bonds with their charges, and for those returning home there was an uncertain future. But it was a necessary change, the last evacuees leaving Northampton at the end of June.

Liberated prisoners of war also began returning to their homes across Northamptonshire over the following weeks, though this was a slow process. There were around 160,000 men held in camps around Germany who could not be moved quickly, or easily, as hostilities ended. But systems were in place to ensure as speedy a return to Britain as was possible. Reception camps had already been set up as receiving centres before the men arrived to help them adjust and prepare them for repatriation with their families. There were also thousands who would need to go through the demobilization process as they returned from combat duty. It would all take time, and there was of course still a war raging in the Far East. By June, Churchill had called a general election.

ARMY BOOK X 801

Surname ...YULE...
Initials ...R.T...
Army No. T/152555

SOLDIER'S RELEASE BOOK

CLASS "A"

> Any person finding this Book is requested to hand it in to any Barracks, Post Office, or Police Station, for transmission to the Under Secretary of State, The War Office, London, S.W.1.

> This book must be presented at the Post Office whenever you cash a postal draft or one of the drafts in your payment book, to enable the Post Office official to record the date of payment on the inside page of the front cover.

S1-5235

A soldier's Release book, received upon 'demob'.

Perhaps surprisingly, it was an election he lost, Labour's Clement Attlee becoming the new Prime Minister on 26 July. He was a new Prime Minister in a new world. By this time the Philippines had been retaken by the Americans, the first atomic bomb test had been carried out in New Mexico and the Vichy French Leader, Petain, had gone on trial. The Americans were gearing up to either attack the Japanese mainland or drop the new atomic bomb on it. As history records, greatly concerned over their own losses so far and the projected casualties likely to be incurred, they opted for the latter. The first atomic bomb was dropped on Hiroshima on 6 August, but did not force the Japanese to surrender; the second, on Nagasaki, did.

Japan's unconditional surrender came on 14 August. Their official and public surrender was carried out on board the USS *Missouri* in Tokyo Bay on 2 September. Three days later, HMS *Sussex* sailed into Singapore harbour unopposed. The war that had engulfed the world was finally over.

CHAPTER EIGHT

Aftermath

From the summer of 1945 to the end of the year, after all the celebrations had died away, there came the realization for many that there was still much to be done. First on the agenda for many across Northamptonshire was the return to civilian life of all those who had joined the forces during the war years. Demobilization, or demob as it became known, actually started within six weeks of the war ending in Europe. The government, under the watchful eye of Minister of Labour Ernest Bevin, set in motion a system by which the armed forces would be gradually reduced and serving personnel returned to their families. The process was straightforward enough. There were two stages for those returning from abroad; firstly a disembarkation centre, essentially a receiving camp, and then a dispersal centre, of which there were nine around the UK, from where the men returned to their homes.

Priority was given to married women, men aged 50 or above and any who possessed key occupational skills that were sorely needed in industry. Fortunately for Northamptonshire, one of the dispersal centres was Talavera Camp on Northampton Racecourse, which helped speed up the process locally. Every man eventually left with a demob suit, two shirts, one pair of shoes, one pair of socks, an appropriate tie, a hat and a coat.

What they were returning to was an uncertain future. Fighting the war had cost vast amounts of money. The country was in debt, and employment – certainly in the short term – was impossible to guarantee. Rationing was still in operation; it remained that way for some considerable time, bread being added to the ration book in the summer of 1946 and potatoes in 1947 after the worst winter weather on record. Normality, or what passed for it, was several years away. Clothes rationing continued until May 1949, petrol rationing until May 1950, sweets and confectionery until February

A mushroom pillbox as it looks today at Grafton Underwood.

1953, sugar to September 1953 and meat – along with all other food rationing – finally ended only in the summer of 1954. There were nine long years during which the county, along with the rest of the country, had to rebuild, reorganize and redevelop in almost every industrial sector.

The process began when the Home Guard was stood down (disbanded on 31 December 1945) and returning servicemen and women went to the polling booths in July 1945. Locally, this was closely followed by an exodus when the Americans and various other foreign troops began to leave areas they had occupied since the mid-point of the war. Knuston Hall, which had served as a transport depot for both the British and Canadian army, returned to its former use, as did Finedon Hall, which had housed the Free French and had been visited by General De Gaulle. Around Rushden, Kettering, Boughton House Park and the various air bases it was a similar story. The USAAF moved out of Polebrook, which finally closed down three years later. Grafton Underwood, Deenethorpe and Chelveston followed on, with Kings Cliffe

All that remains of Grafton Underwood's air raid shelter.

returning to use as a storage depot for the RAF until 1959 when it, too, finally closed. Others went the same way, the land slowly returned to agriculture, until only the odd ruin remained to show there had ever been bombers and fighter aircraft flying out from the county.

Sadly, there were also casualties of peace. Men returning from prison camps across Europe and those who had been held by the Japanese found great difficulty in settling back into Northamptonshire life. There were also the German and Italian prisoners held in the various camps around the county. Many had filled the gaps left in the agricultural workforce when farm workers enlisted in the services, and for some there was no home to return to. Then, of course, there was a whole workforce of women who had stepped in when the war effort demanded more labour. The munition workers, the Women's Land Army, the WVS, the post women, the mechanics, the ATS and those who took over from the men in various factories and machine shops. They found change forced upon them as their jobs began to disappear or be

Grafton Underwood's main runway today.

The memorial at Grafton Underwood.

reclaimed by men returning from the war. For some, these changes were hard to take; for others, the impact of the war had been far more personal. By the end of 1945, many families were still trying to come to terms with the irreplaceable loss of family members during the conflict. Many who had joined the Northamptonshires, enlisted in the Navy or served with the RAF did not return home after VE Day. For these families, change had a different meaning, as it did for thousands of American families mourning the loss of men who had flown the B-17s and Flying Fortresses out of Northamptonshire's air bases.

The war that had come to Northamptonshire had cost the county dear, and when the Northamptonshire Regiment paraded in the town's market square, flanked by huge crowds, on 8 June 1946 to receive the Freedom of the Borough, that thought lingered long in the hearts and minds of all.

Index

Achurch, 75
Admiral Graf Spee, 16
Afrika Korps, 47, 76
Anderson shelter, 2–3, 21, 32
Anderson, Sir John, 2
Anzio, 93, 112
Apethorpe, 75
Ardennes, 31
ARP, 1, 5–6, 26–7, 29, 35, 42, 47, 61–2, 96
Athenia, 14
ATS, 43, 71, 119

Barratt Shoes, 44
Basset-Lowke, 44
Battle of Britain, 35–6, 38
Bedford, 50
Beechener, Cliff, 37
BEF, 14, 16, 28, 30–1, 33
Belgium, 14, 27
Benefield, 10
Berlin, 18, 36, 95, 99, 112
Bevin, Ernest, 117
Bismarck, 48
Bozeat, 54
Brackley, 10, 13, 38, 72, 74
Braun, Eva, 113
Braybrooke, 85
British Timken, 44, 111
Broughton, 67, 71
Bugbrooke, 110
Bugby, Alderman, 55
Burma, 54, 89, 110, 113
Burton Latimer, 7, 31, 60

Calabria, 81
Caroli, Gosta, 37
Casablanca, 71, 73
Castle Ashby, 72
Chamberlain, Neville, 2, 27
Chelveston, 74, 88, 93, 95
Chetwode, Sir Philip, 77
Chipping Norton, 74
Churchill, Sir Winston, 27–8, 30, 38, 49, 52, 66, 71, 81–2, 93, 109, 111
Clopton, 75
Cologne, 61
Conscientious Objectors, 31–2
Corby, 1, 20, 22, 43, 60, 67–8, 105
Coventry, 5, 38
Creaton, 96
Crick, 113
Croughton, 74

Danzig, 2, 10
Daventry, 10, 13, 38, 47, 50, 62, 67, 83, 90, 111
D-Day, 105–106
Deene, 75, 82
Deenethorpe, 74, 82, 93, 95, 106
Denton, 37
Desborough, 7, 31, 38, 60, 78
Doodlebug, 95
Dunkirk, 30, 33, 68
Dunstable, 50
Duston, 35, 44, 110

Earls Barton, 10, 17
Eden, Anthony, 28, 81, 109
Ekins, Joe, 102
El Alamein, 68
Elliot, Walter, 26
Enigma Machine, 48
Express Lift Co, 43

Finedon, 110
Fire Guards, 61
Fire Watchers, 91
France, 2, 8, 10, 14, 24–5, 27–8, 31, 37, 85, 95, 101, 105

Gable, Clark, 79
Gallay, Betty, 70
Geddington, 42, 85
Glenn, Alderman, 25
Gort, Lord, 14
Göring, Herman, 36
Gneisenau, 59
Grafton Underwood, 62–3, 74, 93
Glyndwr, Michael, 76
Great Harrowden, 109
Greece, 8, 48, 76
Gretton, 67

Harrington, 91
Harris, Air Marshal Arthur, 61, 74, 82
Higham Ferrers, 12, 38, 47, 56, 60, 111
Hirohito, 59
Hiroshima, 116
Hitler, Adolf, 2, 4, 8, 10, 17, 27–8, 30, 35, 40, 48, 50, 52, 54, 59, 74, 77, 81, 94–5, 97, 109, 113

HMS *Achilles*, 16
HMS *Ajax*, 16
HMS *Ark Royal*, 15, 48
HMS *Bulldog*, 48
HMS *Courageous*, 14
HMS *Duke of York*, 84
HMS *Exeter*, 16
HMS *Hood*, 48
HMS *Prince of Wales*, 52
HMS *Repulse*, 52
HMS *Sussex*, 116
Holland, 27–8
Homeguard, 28, 37, 42, 47, 52, 56, 65, 69, 72, 86, 97, 101, 118
Howard, Leslie, 26, 76

IRA, 5
Irchester, 47, 50
Irthlingborough, 47, 54, 59, 69
Isham, 59
Islip, 1

Johnson, Amy, 46
Joyce, William, 18

Keeler, Christine, 23
Kettering, 4–5, 7, 10, 13, 16–17, 20–1, 23, 26, 31, 33, 38, 42, 44, 46, 49, 54, 57, 60, 62, 69, 79, 86, 90, 97, 102, 106, 114, 118
Kettering Hospital, 27, 83
Kings Cliffe, 71, 90, 101
Kislingbury, 113

Lamport, 75
Langsdorff, Hans, 16
Leicester, 31
Leighton Buzzard, 50

Lilford, 75
London, 8, 36, 61, 96
Lord Haw Haw, 18
Luftwaffe, 27, 35, 42, 47–8, 56, 61, 63
Lyveden, 75

Madgwick, Flt Sgt, 50
Maginot Line, 24, 28
Maison De Convalescence, 68
Malaya, 54
Martin, Maj, 76
Military Training Act, 8
Miller, Glen, 101
Ministry of Agriculture, 60
Ministry of Food, 12, 69
Ministry of Labour, 58
Mitchell, Jeanne, 68
Mitford, Diana, 17–19
Mitford, Unity, 17–19
Mollison, Jim, 46
Montevideo, 16
Montgomery, Bernard, 66, 71, 73, 76, 81, 88, 102
Morrison, Herbert, 56
Moulton, 49
Munich, 2, 4
Mussolini, 8, 33, 40, 48, 77, 81, 111, 113

Nagasaki, 114
National Registration Bill, 13
National Service Act, 58
National Service Committee, 6
New Guinea, 54, 69
North Africa, 40, 47, 68, 71, 83
Northampton, 7, 13, 16, 21–3, 26–7, 31, 43, 47, 50, 55, 57, 75, 83, 90, 98–9, 102, 104, 110–11, 114
Northampton, Lord, 37
Northampton Regt, 1, 6, 16, 19, 24, 31, 37, 56, 66, 72, 87, 89, 99, 110

Oakington, 50
Observer Corps, 6, 8, 43, 101
Olney, 10
Operation Barbarosa, 52
Operation Dragoon, 96
Operation Mincemeat, 76
Operation Varsity, 110
Orton, CSM, 56
Oundle, 10, 13, 42, 60, 75

Paris, 31, 96
Paterson, William, 2
Patton, Gen, 102
Paulerspury, 49, 67
Pearl Harbor, 52
Peenemunde, 99
Petacci, Clara, 113
Peterborough, 74, 106
Phoney War, 17, 19, 27
Pickard, Group Capt Percy, 90
Poland, 2, 8, 10
Powell, Lord Baden, 46
Profumo, John, 4, 23–4

RAF, 6, 8, 25, 27, 31, 35–6, 43–4, 46, 52, 61, 71–2, 74, 82, 86–7, 89–90, 93–4, 101, 106, 119, 122
Raunds, 7, 10, 60, 89, 107
Reichstag, 4, 10
Riverplate, Battle of, 16

Rommel, Erwin, 4, 7, 62, 68, 73
Roosevelt, Franklin D., 4, 49, 55, 71, 81, 93, 109, 112
Rothwell, 7, 23, 31, 38, 60, 91
Rushden, 5, 7, 31, 38, 47, 50, 62, 67, 87, 106, 110–11, 118

Sandy, 50
Scaldwell, 113
Scharnhorst, 59, 84
Sears & Co., 96
Sicily, 76
Silverstone, 74
Simon, Sir John, 26
Singapore, 52
Solomon Islands, 54, 76
Spratton, 75
Spriggs, Cyril, 89
Stewarts and Lloyds, 43, 105
Sumpter, Arthur, 70
Sywell, 44

Tansor, 75
Tebbutt, Mr, 72–3
Thrapston, 13, 38, 59, 80
Tirpitz, 101
Titchmarsh, 61
Tolstoy, Alexei, 77–8
Towcester, 13, 38
Tresham Hall, 4
Truman, Harry S., 112
Tubby Turner, 54

U-boat, 14, 48, 60, 71–3, 100
USAAF, 62, 71, 74–5, 85, 93, 104, 109, 118

V1 Rocket, 97, 111
V2 Rocket, 97, 99, 111
VE Day, 113–14, 122
Vienna, 18
Von Ribbentrop, 10

WAAF, 43
Wake, Maj Gen, 29
Walgrave, 67
Wallis and Linnell, 43
Warmington, 62, 109
Wavell, Gen Archibald, 40
Weldon, 47, 106
Wellingborough, 7, 13, 21, 29, 33, 38, 42, 50, 54, 57, 59, 62, 64–5, 69, 83, 98, 102, 104, 108, 114
Weston Favell, 105
White, John, 56, 111
Winfield, R.A., 7
Wittman, Michael, 102
Wollaston, 20
Women's Auxilliary Police, 58
Women's Land Army, 5, 45, 60, 67, 119
Woodford, 31, 48
WRNS, 43
WVS, 1, 19, 41–2, 49, 60, 83, 119

Yamamoto, Adml, 76
Yardley Hastings, 37
Yelden, 88

Zeppelin, 2